Learning LIBRARY
Math

grade 1

The basic skills your 1st grader needs!

- **Addition & Subtraction**
- **Measurement**
- **Geometry**
- **Algebra & Functions**
- **Graphing**

- **Fractions**
- **Time & Money**
- **Patterns**
- **Probability**
- **Problem Solving**

Editor: Kathy Wolf
Contributing Writer: Darcy Brown
Copy Editors: Tracy Johnson, Carol Rawleigh
Contributing Artist: Cathy Spangler Bruce
Typesetters: Lynette Dickerson, Mark Rainey
Cover Illustration and Design: Nick Greenwood

Manufactured in the United States
10 9 8 7 6 5 4 3 2 1

Table of Contents

Numbers and Operations

First graders spend a big part of their school year learning about numbers and the operations of addition and subtraction. They develop what is called *number sense* and begin to use numbers mentally. In first grade, your child will learn to

- investigate numbers using *manipulatives* such as beans or counters
- compare numbers singly and in sets
- use vocabulary and symbols for *greater than, less than,* and *equal to* when comparing numbers
- add and subtract to 18

When learning to add numbers, your child will be taught to group manipulatives into sets, then put the sets together, and finally count the manipulatives to find the sum. First graders should also be able to make a set and take away from the set to subtract.

Your child will use addition and subtraction to solve simple *word problems.* He'll be able to make up his own problems too.

To work with larger numbers, your child will need to understand *place value.* This means that he knows that the arrangement of numbers or the "place" of a number determines how much it is worth. For example, in the number 28 the digit 8 is in the ones place and the digit 2 is in the tens place, so this number means 2 tens and 8 ones.

Once a first grader understands place value, he can
- use base-ten blocks to build numbers to 100
- use a hundreds board to explore number order
- count to 100 by 2s, 5s, and 10s
- identify odd and even numbers
- follow a skip-counting pattern
- identify numbers that come *before, after,* or *between* two numbers

Key Math Skills for Grade 1
Numbers and Operations

- Comparing sets greater than, less than, and equal to (>, <, =)

- Connecting number words, numerals, and sets to 10

- Addition facts to 20

- Subtraction facts to 20

- Fact families to 18

- Column addition: three one-digit numbers

- Number order: numerals before and after

- Place value: tens and ones to 100

- Number order: counting to 100

- Number order: counting by 2s, 5s, and 10s to 100

Name _____

Tweet Treats

This bird is hungry.
He wants to eat the **big** set.

Circle the **big** set.

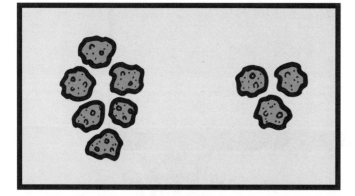

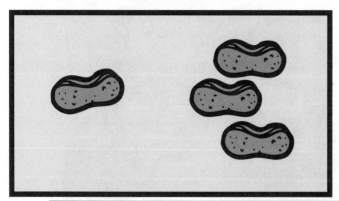
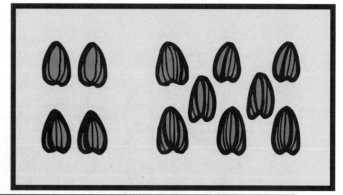

At Home: Provide peanuts, sunflower seeds, or candy corn for your child to group to make sets. Ask your first grader to compare and tell you which set is greater than or less than your set.

6

Name _____

Number Munching

The bird eats the **big** number.
Trace the bird's mouth.

> means **greater than**.   < means **less than**.

Look at the numbers below.
Write > or < in each circle.

3 **<** 7	8 ◯ 6	2 ◯ 4
5 ◯ 4	2 ◯ 3	7 ◯ 5
3 ◯ 6	5 ◯ 2	9 ◯ 8
7 ◯ 9	4 ◯ 0	2 ◯ 6

Name _____

Winter Snacks

Trace.

8 > 5

4 < 7

Write > or < in each circle.

5	◯	9	6	◯	4	2	◯	8
6	◯	5	9	◯	1	8	◯	7
2	◯	4	1	◯	2	5	◯	2
9	◯	4	3	◯	9	1	◯	3
6	◯	3	5	◯	7	8	◯	5

Equal Eating

Sometimes numbers are the same.
They are **equal.**

_____ = _____

= means **is the same as.**   Write the numbers above.

Write >, <, or = in each circle.

8 ◯ 4	0 ◯ 7	4 ◯ 4
3 ◯ 3	6 ◯ 6	7 ◯ 8
5 ◯ 5	2 ◯ 5	6 ◯ 4
7 ◯ 4	3 ◯ 0	9 ◯ 9
6 ◯ 9	2 ◯ 2	4 ◯ 2

At Home: Provide sunflower seeds for your child to manipulate to make sets equal to those you create. Help your first grader write the number sentence using the symbols >, <, or =. Then eat the equal sets or feed them to the birds!

Making a Beeline

Count.
Write.
Draw a line to match.

| one |
| four |
| ten |
| two |
| five |
| three |
| eight |
| six |
| nine |
| seven |

Name _____

More Pizza, Please!

Count.
Add.

1.

2 + 3 = _____

2.

4 + 1 = _____

3.

1 + 3 = _____

4.

3 + 3 = _____

5.

5 + 1 = _____

6.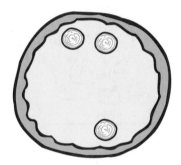

2 + 1 = _____

7.

3 + 0 = _____

8.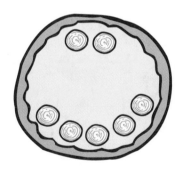

2 + 5 = _____

9.

3 + 4 = _____

Draw to match.
Add.

10.

4 + 2 = _____

11.

6 + 1 = _____

11

Pups in Line

Cut.
Glue to match.

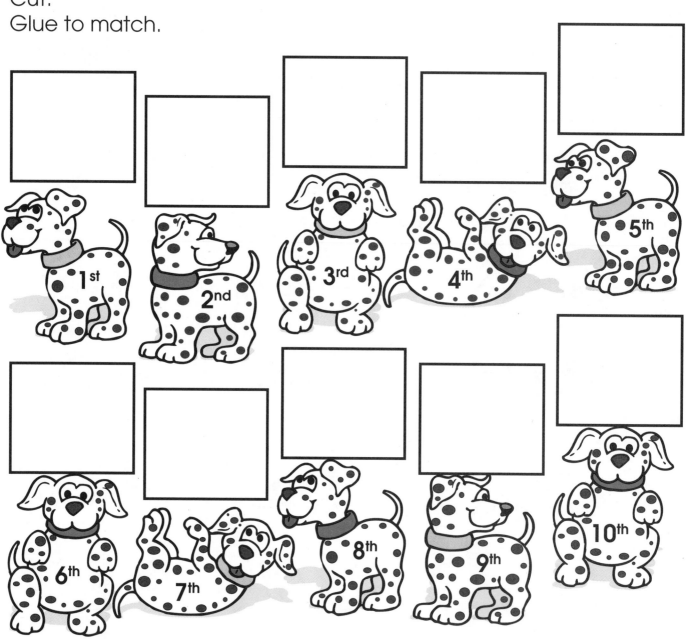

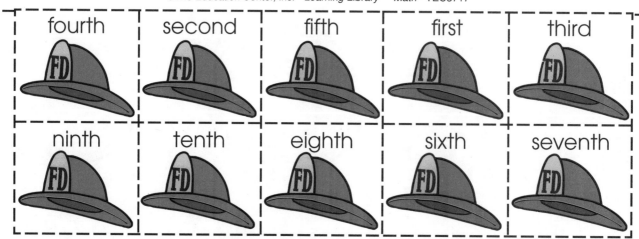

Seashell Symphony

Add.

$$2 + 3$$

$$4 + 2$$

$$2 + 2$$

$$1 + 4$$

$$1 + 0$$

$$2 + 1$$

$$3 + 3$$

$$0 + 4$$

$$0 + 3$$

$$1 + 5$$

$$0 + 5$$

$$3 + 2$$

$$1 + 3$$

$$0 + 6$$

At Home: Provide seashells or shell pasta to count and add sets.

Name _____

Add.

Treasure Under the Sea

5
+ 2
_____

4
+ 1
_____

5
+ 0
_____

1
+ 6
_____

6
+ 1
_____

3
+ 1
_____

2
+ 1
_____

2
+ 4
_____

2
+ 0
_____

4
+ 3
_____

2
+ 5
_____

1
+ 1
_____

5
+ 1
_____

0
+ 6
_____

7
+ 0
_____

3
+ 4
_____

Name _____

Sea Horses, Swim!

Add.

4 + 4 = ____   6 + 1 = ____   5 + 2 = ____   0 + 8 = ____

4 + 3 = ____   5 + 3 = ____   1 + 7 = ____   6 + 2 = ____

0 + 5 = ____   2 + 5 = ____   2 + 6 = ____   3 + 5 = ____

8 + 0 = ____   3 + 4 = ____   0 + 7 = ____   7 + 1 = ____

Name _____

Go for the Goal

Add.
Complete the code to solve the riddle.

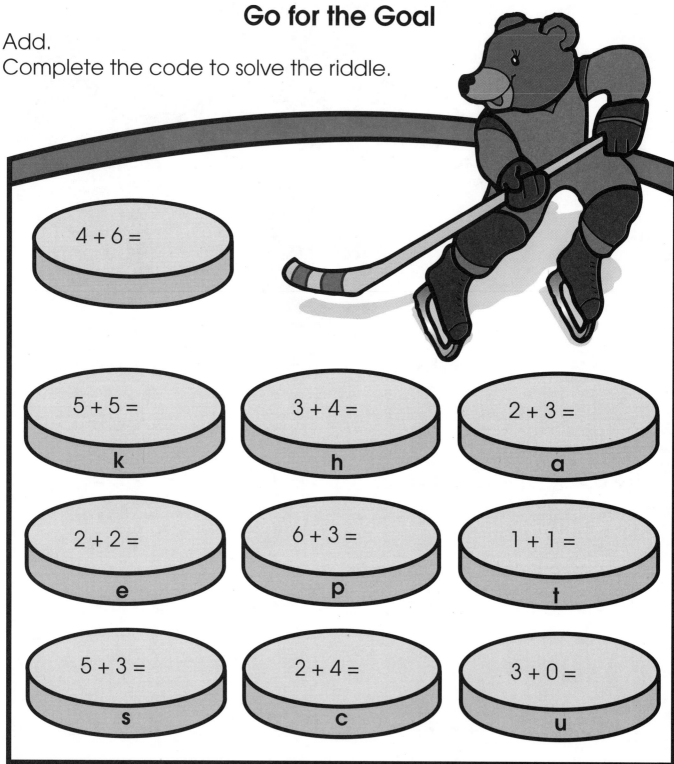

4 + 6 =

5 + 5 = **k**

3 + 4 = **h**

2 + 3 = **a**

2 + 2 = **e**

6 + 3 = **p**

1 + 1 = **t**

5 + 3 = **s**

2 + 4 = **c**

3 + 0 = **u**

Riddle: Are hockey players polite?
Answer: Yes, because they always

___ ___ ___ ___   ___ ___ ___   ___ ___ ___ ___!
 9   5   8   8   2   7   4   9   3   6   10

Name _____

Snowshoe Shuffle

Subtract.
Complete the code to solve the riddle.

Riddle: Why did the bear snowshoe over the mountain?

Answer:

___ ___   ___ **e** **e**   ___ ___ ___ ___
5   2   4   1   9 10   5

___ **e**   ___ ___ ___ ___ ___   ___ **e** **e**
9   8   2   6   7   3   4

Name_____

Cars and Trucks

Subtract.
Color by the code.

Color Code:

1 = red   2 = blue
3 = yellow   4 = green

$$\begin{array}{r} 6 \\ -\ 3 \\ \hline \end{array}$$

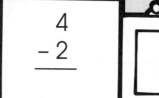

$$\begin{array}{r} 4 \\ -\ 2 \\ \hline \end{array}$$

$$\begin{array}{r} 5 \\ -\ 4 \\ \hline \end{array}$$

5 – 1 = _____

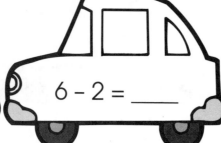

6 – 2 = _____

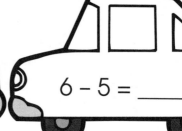

6 – 5 = _____

$$\begin{array}{r} 6 \\ -\ 4 \\ \hline \end{array}$$

$$\begin{array}{r} 5 \\ -\ 2 \\ \hline \end{array}$$

$$\begin{array}{r} 4 \\ -\ 3 \\ \hline \end{array}$$

At Home: Gather seven toy cars or trucks to use as counters. Have your child group the cars into sets and take away from each set to work the subtraction problems.

Name_____

Take to the Air

Subtract.
Color by the code.

Color Code:

1 = orange	2 = brown
3 = green	4 = yellow
5 = blue	6 = red

Row 1:
6 − 3   6 − 1   7 − 4

Row 2:
5 − 3   7 − 1   7 − 2

Row 3:
6 − 2   4 − 3   7 − 5

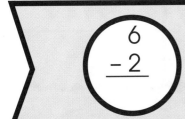

Row 4:
7 − 6   6 − 4   7 − 3

At Home: Provide cotton balls to use as "cloud" counters. Have your child make sets of clouds and take away clouds to work additional subtraction problems.

Boats Afloat

Subtract.
Color by the code.

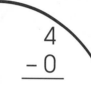
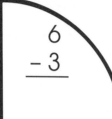
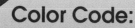

Color Code:

	3 = green
4 = red	5 = blue
6 = yellow	7 = orange

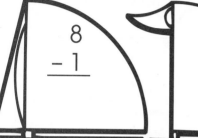

$$\begin{array}{r} 8 \\ -1 \\ \hline \end{array}$$

$$\begin{array}{r} 4 \\ -0 \\ \hline \end{array}$$

$$\begin{array}{r} 6 \\ -3 \\ \hline \end{array}$$

$$\begin{array}{r} 8 \\ -5 \\ \hline \end{array}$$

$$\begin{array}{r} 7 \\ -0 \\ \hline \end{array}$$

$$\begin{array}{r} 8 \\ -2 \\ \hline \end{array}$$

$$\begin{array}{r} 6 \\ -1 \\ \hline \end{array}$$

$$\begin{array}{r} 7 \\ -1 \\ \hline \end{array}$$

$$\begin{array}{r} 8 \\ -4 \\ \hline \end{array}$$

$$\begin{array}{r} 7 \\ -4 \\ \hline \end{array}$$

$$\begin{array}{r} 5 \\ -2 \\ \hline \end{array}$$

$$\begin{array}{r} 8 \\ -3 \\ \hline \end{array}$$

At Home: Create eight sailboats by floating 8 corks or 8 lemons in a tub of water. Allow your child to float the number of boats in each set and subtract or take away from the set to solve the problems above.

Name_____

Subtraction Train

Subtract.
Color by the code.

Color Code:

2 and 3 = yellow
4 and 5 = blue
6 and 7 = green
8 and 9 = red

9 − 6	8 − 2	8 − 1	9 − 4

8 − 3	6 − 2	9 − 0	9 − 1

7 − 1	9 − 2	7 − 0	8 − 4

9 − 5	9 − 7	9 − 3	8 − 0

At Home: All aboard the Cheese Choo-choo for subtraction practice. Provide cheese cubes for your child to use as manipulative counters. Work the problems and then eat the cargo!

Name_____

Skating Away

Subtract.
Color by the code.

10 − 6	9 − 1	10 − 0

6 − 3	**Color Code:**

Color Code:
3 and 4 = yellow   5 and 6 = green
7 and 8 = blue   9 and 10 = red

8 − 4	10 − 2	9 − 5	10 − 7

At Home: Review subtraction to ten by counting out ten pennies. Have your child make sets of pennies and take away pennies to work the problems above.

			5 − 2

10 − 1	9 − 0	8 − 3	10 − 4

7 − 4		

	9 − 6	10 − 3

Take Some Tortillas

Add.
Color.

Color Code	7 and 8 = brown	9 and 10 = yellow

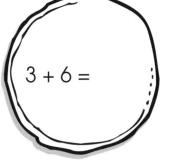

3 + 6 =

5 + 2 =

4 + 6 =

3 + 5 =

7 + 3 =

4 + 4 =

2 + 7 =

6 + 1 =

5 + 4 =

3 + 4 =

5 + 5 =

2 + 6 =

Tortillas are made with corn flour.

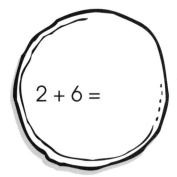

Name_____

Add Chilies and Filling

Add.
Color.

Color Code	
10 =	red
9 =	green
8 =	yellow
7 =	orange

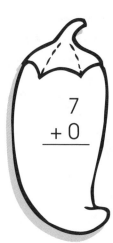
7
+0

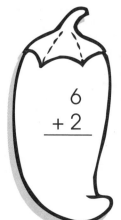
6
+2

1
+8

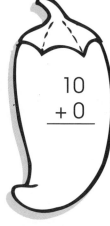
10
+0

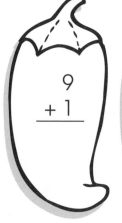
9
+1

8
+1

2
+5

7
+1

6
+3

8
+2

6
+4

7
+2

4
+3

5
+3

4
+5

3
+7

Chili peppers are very hot!

Queso and Tomato Topping

Subtract.
Color.

4 = green	5 = red	6 = yellow	7 = orange

 6 − 0 =

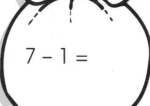 8 − 3 =

 9 − 5 =

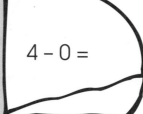 5 − 1 =

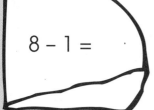 9 − 4 =

 7 − 1 =

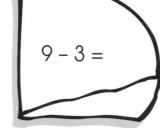 4 − 0 =

 7 − 0 =

8 − 1 =

6 − 2 =

 9 − 3 =

7 − 2 =

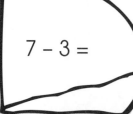 7 − 3 =

 9 − 2 =

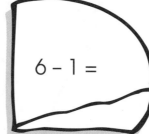 6 − 1 =

 8 − 2 =

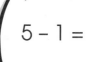

Queso means cheese in Spanish.

Name_____

Tortilla Chips and Dip

Subtract.
Color.

1, 2, 3 = red	4, 5, 6 = yellow	7, 8 = orange

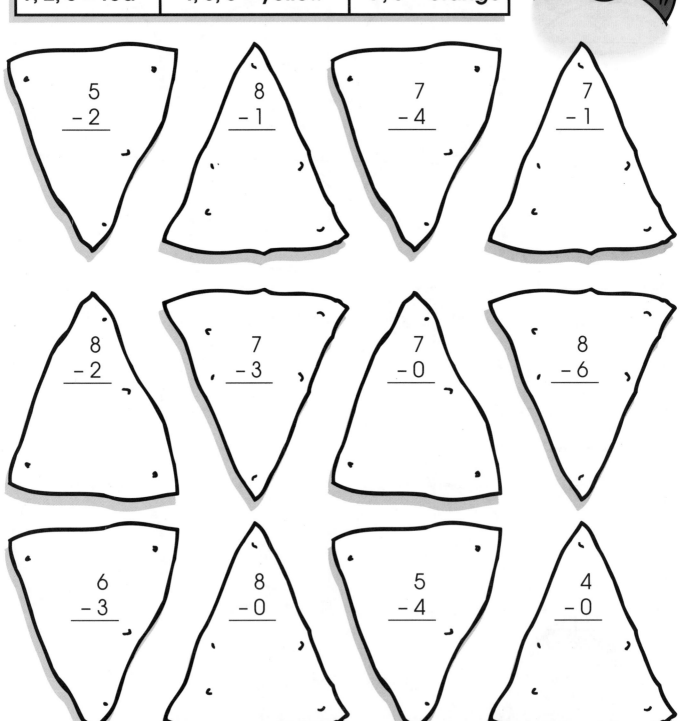

Row 1:
- 5 − 2
- 8 − 1
- 7 − 4
- 7 − 1

Row 2:
- 8 − 2
- 7 − 3
- 7 − 0
- 8 − 6

Row 3:
- 6 − 3
- 8 − 0
- 5 − 4
- 4 − 0

At Home: Make up subtraction problems to 8 for your child to solve using tortilla chips as manipulatives!

Cool Quesadillas

Subtract.
Color.

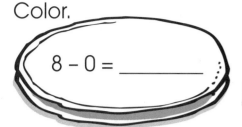
$8 - 0 =$ _____

$9 - 3 =$ _____

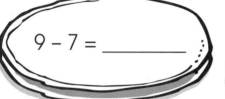
$9 - 7 =$ _____

$9 - 5 =$ _____

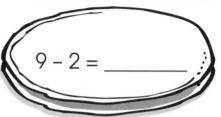
$9 - 2 =$ _____

$7 - 0 =$ _____

$7 - 1 =$ _____

$6 - 2 =$ _____

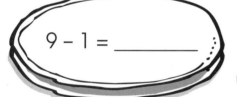
$9 - 1 =$ _____

$8 - 4 =$ _____

$9 - 0 =$ _____

$8 - 3 =$ _____

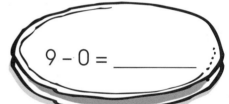
$8 - 1 =$ _____

$9 - 4 =$ _____

$9 - 6 =$ _____

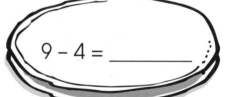
$8 - 2 =$ _____

At Home: Bring home a menu from a Mexican restaurant. Use the items on the menu to create subtraction problems. (Papa ordered ten tacos. He ate five. How many are left? Write the number sentence.)

Tacos...Ta-dah!

Subtract.
Color.

6 and 7 = yellow	5 and 8 = brown
4 and 9 = blue	3 and 10 = orange

10
− 0

10
− 2

9
− 1

6
− 3

8
− 0

9
− 0

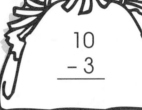
10
− 3

5
− 0

8
− 4

10
− 4

9
− 5

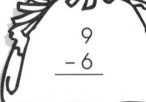
9
− 6

8
− 5

10
− 1

5
− 2

7
− 4

A taco is totally tasty!

Name_____

Bon Voyage!

The ship is in port.
It is going on a voyage.
Add.

The ship has **6** sailors.
4 more sailors come aboard.
How many sailors are on the ship?

There are _____ sailors.

There are **5** upper bunk beds.
There are **4** lower bunk beds.
How many bunk beds in all?

There are _____ bunk beds.

The sailors hoist **3** sails.
They hoist **3** more sails.
How many sails are there?

There are _____ sails.

There are **6** boxes of crackers.
There are **2** boxes of jerky.
How many boxes of food in all?

There are _____ boxes.

The ship sails to Shell Island to get water.
Add.

Sal gets **3** jugs of water.
Pete gets **7** jugs of water.
How many jugs in all?

There are _____ jugs of water.

Captain Kidd drinks **5** cups of water.
He drinks **2** more cups of water.
How many cups does he drink?

He drinks _____ cups of water.

Ahab gets **4** buckets of water.
Sukey gets **5** buckets of water.
How many buckets in all?

There are _____ buckets.

Pol Parrot takes **8** sips of water.
She takes **1** more sip of water.
How many sips does she take?

She takes _____ sips.

Ahoy, Matey!
Make a list!

At Home: Ask your child to make a list of what he or she would take on a voyage and write how many of each item.

Animal Island Sights

The ship sails from Shell Island
   to Animal Island.
The sailors see many animals!
Add or subtract.

Pete sees **10** parrots.
He sees **5** parrots fly away.
How many parrots are left?

There are _____ parrots left.

Jack sees **2** tigers in the grass.
He sees **8** tigers in the bushes.
How many tigers does he see?

Jack sees _____ tigers.

Bill sees **7** monkey babies.
He sees **7** monkey babies run away.
How many babies are left?

There are _____ babies left.

Nell sees **8** snakes.
She sees **4** snakes slide away.
How many snakes are left?

There are _____ snakes left.

Sal sees **6** brown monkeys.
She sees **3** black monkeys.
How many monkeys does she see?

Sal sees _____ monkeys.

Annie sees **9** dolphins.
She sees **7** dolphins swim away.
How many dolphins are left?

There are _____ dolphins left.

Nancy sees **2** baby elephants.
She sees **4** mother elephants.
How many elephants does she see?

Nancy sees _____ elephants.

Tom sees **10** crocodiles.
He sees **2** crocodiles crawl away.
How many crocodiles are left?

There are _____ crocodiles left.

There are 3 monkeys in the trees.   How many monkeys in all?
There are 3 monkeys on the ground.
There are 3 monkeys in the water.   There are _____ monkeys.

**Avast, Matey!
Count with crackers!**

At Home: Work the problems together with animal crackers.

Shipshape Stop

The ship sails from Animal Island to Shipwreck Island.
The sailors check their ship.
Add.

A sail has **6** holes on one side.
It has **6** holes on the other side.
How many holes are in the sail?

There are _____ holes.

Abby cleans **9** portholes.
Ben cleans **3** portholes.
How many did they clean?

They cleaned _____ portholes.

There are **4** full water jugs.
There are **3** empty water jugs.
How many water jugs in all?

There are _____ water jugs.

There are **3** new mops.
There are **8** old mops.
How many mops in all?

There are _____ mops.

Check the ship's cargo. Fill in the blanks.

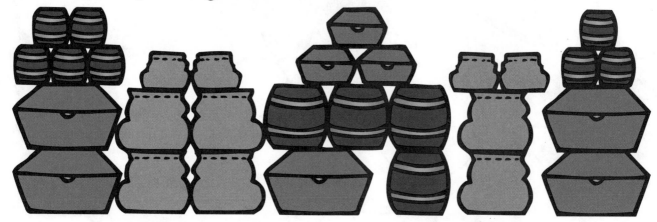

_____ small sacks

_____ big sacks

_____ sacks in all

_____ small barrels

_____ big barrels

_____ barrels in all

_____ small chests

_____ big chests

_____ chests in all

Arrgh, Matey!
Fill a chest!

At Home: Pack a picnic lunch for the family. Together, count the number of items as you place them in the basket.

Name _____

Buzzing Into Addition

Add.
Color by the code.

$$\begin{array}{r} 2 \\ +10 \\ \hline \end{array}$$

$$\begin{array}{r} 4 \\ +6 \\ \hline \end{array}$$

$$\begin{array}{r} 5 \\ +7 \\ \hline \end{array}$$

$$\begin{array}{r} 2 \\ +7 \\ \hline \end{array}$$

$$\begin{array}{r} 8 \\ +3 \\ \hline \end{array}$$

$$\begin{array}{r} 3 \\ +9 \\ \hline \end{array}$$

$$\begin{array}{r} 4 \\ +5 \\ \hline \end{array}$$

$$\begin{array}{r} 6 \\ +6 \\ \hline \end{array}$$

$$\begin{array}{r} 8 \\ +4 \\ \hline \end{array}$$

$$\begin{array}{r} 3 \\ +6 \\ \hline \end{array}$$

$$\begin{array}{r} 4 \\ +8 \\ \hline \end{array}$$

$$\begin{array}{r} 3 \\ +7 \\ \hline \end{array}$$

$$\begin{array}{r} 2 \\ +9 \\ \hline \end{array}$$

$$\begin{array}{r} 11 \\ +1 \\ \hline \end{array}$$

$$\begin{array}{r} 10 \\ +2 \\ \hline \end{array}$$

Color Code

9 = purple   10 = orange   11 = yellow   12 = red

At Home: Make bumblebee counters from yellow pom-poms to work the problems.

Busy Queen Bee

Add.
Subtract.
Color.

Color Code		
7 = **purple**	8 = **red**	9 = **brown**
10 = **pink**	11 = **orange**	12 = **yellow**

$$3 + 7$$ $$9 + 3$$ $$12 - 5$$ $$10 - 2$$

$$12 - 3$$ $$5 + 6$$ $$6 + 6$$ $$10 - 1$$

$$12 - 4$$ $$10 + 2$$ $$8 + 3$$ $$11 - 4$$

Queenie's Honeycomb

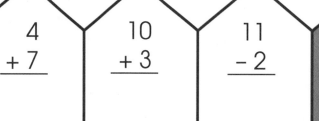

Add.
Subtract.
Color.

Color Code
9 and 10 = **brown**
11 and 12 = **orange**
13 and 14 = **yellow**

4
+ 7

10
+ 3

11
− 2

9
+ 5

14
− 5

6
+ 4

8
+ 6

5
+ 4

12
− 3

7
+ 5

7
+ 7

13
− 4

9
− 0

5
+ 8

Queen Bee's Best

Read each box.
Add or subtract.

Queen Bee's Best Honey

9 🐝 s buzz.	☐
2 more buzz.	+ ☐
How many in all?	☐

2 🐝 s fly.	☐
7 more fly.	+ ☐
How many in all?	☐

5 🐝 s sit.	☐
5 more sit.	+ ☐
How many in all?	☐

11 🐝 s sit.	☐
8 fly away.	− ☐
How many left?	☐

8 🐝 s buzz.	☐
4 fly away.	− ☐
How many left?	☐

11 🐝 s sit.	☐
4 fly away.	− ☐
How many left?	☐

At Home: Use the bumblebee counters from page 32 to work the problems.
Or try honey graham cracker shapes.

Name _____

Home Sweet Hive

Read each box.
Add or subtract.

Queenie has 6 s.

She gets 7 more s.

She has [13] s in all.

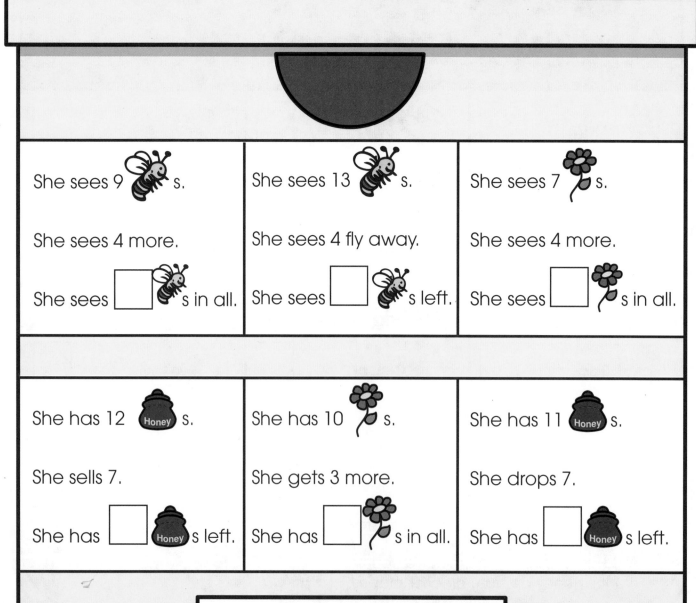

She sees 9 🐝s.

She sees 4 more.

She sees [ ] 🐝s in all.

She sees 13 🐝s.

She sees 4 fly away.

She sees [ ] 🐝s left.

She sees 7 🌼s.

She sees 4 more.

She sees [ ] 🌼s in all.

She has 12 Honeys.

She sells 7.

She has [ ] Honeys left.

She has 10 🌼s.

She gets 3 more.

She has [ ] 🌼s in all.

She has 11 Honeys.

She drops 7.

She has [ ] Honeys left.

36

Name _____

Fact Family Tree

Write each answer.

6 + 7 = _____

7 + 6 = _____

13 – 6 = _____

13 – 7 = _____

9 + 7 = _____

7 + 9 = _____

16 – 9 = _____

16 – 7 = _____

4 + 8 = _____

8 + 4 = _____

12 – 4 = _____

12 – 8 = _____

8 + 9 = _____

9 + 8 = _____

17 – 9 = _____

17 – 8 = _____

8 + 7 = _____

7 + 8 = _____

15 – 7 = _____

15 – 8 = _____

9 + 9 = _____

18 – 9 = _____

5 + 7 = _____

7 + 5 = _____

12 – 5 = _____

12 – 7 = _____

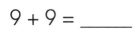

At Home: Have your child draw a tree on another sheet of paper by tracing his or her hand and forearm to make branches. On each branch have him write a fact from a fact family such as 6 + 7, 7 + 6, 13 – 6, 13 – 7.

Hill-Climbing Cars

Add.
Color by the code.

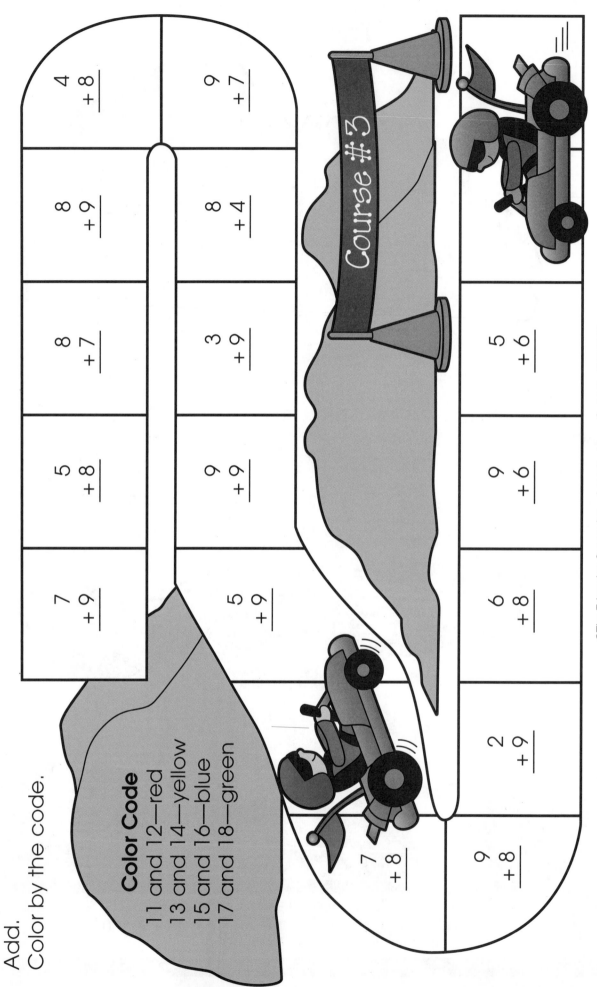

Color Code
11 and 12—red
13 and 14—yellow
15 and 16—blue
17 and 18—green

$$\begin{array}{r}7\\+9\\\hline\end{array}$$
$$\begin{array}{r}5\\+8\\\hline\end{array}$$
$$\begin{array}{r}8\\+7\\\hline\end{array}$$
$$\begin{array}{r}8\\+9\\\hline\end{array}$$
$$\begin{array}{r}4\\+8\\\hline\end{array}$$

$$\begin{array}{r}5\\+9\\\hline\end{array}$$
$$\begin{array}{r}9\\+9\\\hline\end{array}$$
$$\begin{array}{r}3\\+9\\\hline\end{array}$$
$$\begin{array}{r}8\\+4\\\hline\end{array}$$
$$\begin{array}{r}9\\+7\\\hline\end{array}$$

Course #3

$$\begin{array}{r}2\\+9\\\hline\end{array}$$
$$\begin{array}{r}6\\+8\\\hline\end{array}$$
$$\begin{array}{r}9\\+6\\\hline\end{array}$$
$$\begin{array}{r}5\\+6\\\hline\end{array}$$

$$\begin{array}{r}9\\+8\\\hline\end{array}$$
$$\begin{array}{r}7\\+8\\\hline\end{array}$$

Name

Revving Up and Ready!

Add or subtract.
Color by the code.

Color Code
6 and 7—red
8 and 9—yellow
15 and 16—blue
17 and 18—green

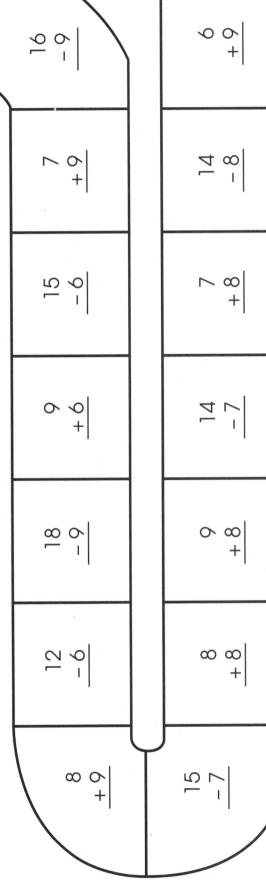

Course #4

$$\begin{array}{r} 9 \\ +9 \\ \hline \end{array}$$

$$\begin{array}{r} 17 \\ -9 \\ \hline \end{array}$$

$$\begin{array}{r} 16 \\ -9 \\ \hline \end{array}$$

$$\begin{array}{r} 6 \\ +9 \\ \hline \end{array}$$

$$\begin{array}{r} 7 \\ +9 \\ \hline \end{array}$$

$$\begin{array}{r} 14 \\ -8 \\ \hline \end{array}$$

$$\begin{array}{r} 15 \\ -6 \\ \hline \end{array}$$

$$\begin{array}{r} 7 \\ +8 \\ \hline \end{array}$$

$$\begin{array}{r} 9 \\ +6 \\ \hline \end{array}$$

$$\begin{array}{r} 14 \\ -7 \\ \hline \end{array}$$

$$\begin{array}{r} 18 \\ -9 \\ \hline \end{array}$$

$$\begin{array}{r} 9 \\ +8 \\ \hline \end{array}$$

$$\begin{array}{r} 12 \\ -6 \\ \hline \end{array}$$

$$\begin{array}{r} 8 \\ +8 \\ \hline \end{array}$$

$$\begin{array}{r} 8 \\ +9 \\ \hline \end{array}$$

$$\begin{array}{r} 15 \\ -7 \\ \hline \end{array}$$

40 Name _____

Add.
Color by the code.

The Winner!

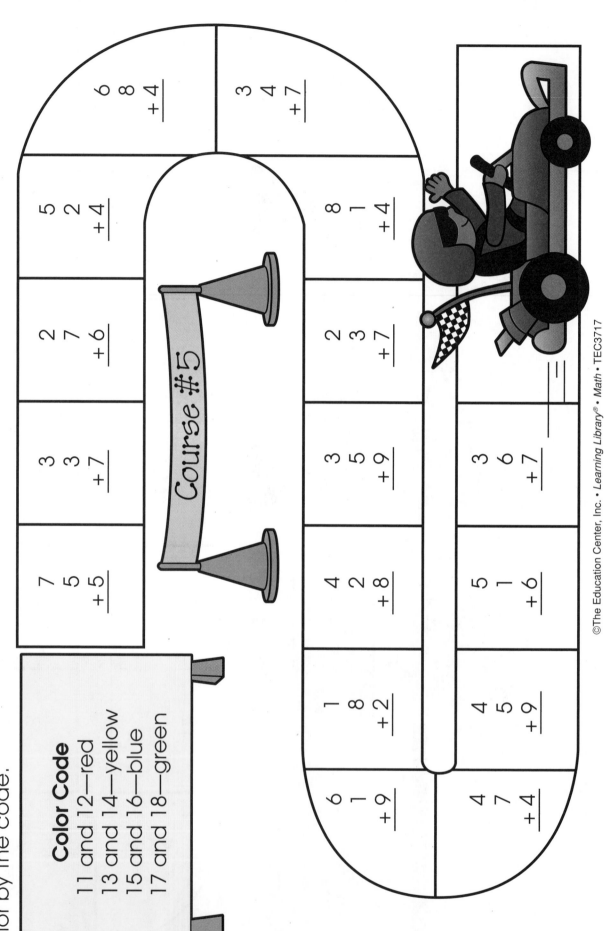

Color Code
11 and 12—red
13 and 14—yellow
15 and 16—blue
17 and 18—green

Course #5

$$\begin{array}{r} 6 \\ 8 \\ +4 \\ \hline \end{array}$$

$$\begin{array}{r} 3 \\ 4 \\ +7 \\ \hline \end{array}$$

$$\begin{array}{r} 5 \\ 2 \\ +4 \\ \hline \end{array}$$

$$\begin{array}{r} 8 \\ 1 \\ +4 \\ \hline \end{array}$$

$$\begin{array}{r} 2 \\ 7 \\ +6 \\ \hline \end{array}$$

$$\begin{array}{r} 2 \\ 3 \\ +7 \\ \hline \end{array}$$

$$\begin{array}{r} 3 \\ 3 \\ +7 \\ \hline \end{array}$$

$$\begin{array}{r} 3 \\ 5 \\ +9 \\ \hline \end{array}$$

$$\begin{array}{r} 3 \\ 6 \\ +7 \\ \hline \end{array}$$

$$\begin{array}{r} 7 \\ 5 \\ +5 \\ \hline \end{array}$$

$$\begin{array}{r} 4 \\ 2 \\ +8 \\ \hline \end{array}$$

$$\begin{array}{r} 5 \\ 1 \\ +6 \\ \hline \end{array}$$

$$\begin{array}{r} 1 \\ 8 \\ +2 \\ \hline \end{array}$$

$$\begin{array}{r} 4 \\ 5 \\ +9 \\ \hline \end{array}$$

$$\begin{array}{r} 6 \\ 1 \\ +9 \\ \hline \end{array}$$

$$\begin{array}{r} 4 \\ 7 \\ +4 \\ \hline \end{array}$$

Name _____

Cozy Cave

Write the number that comes **before**.
Write the number that comes **after**.

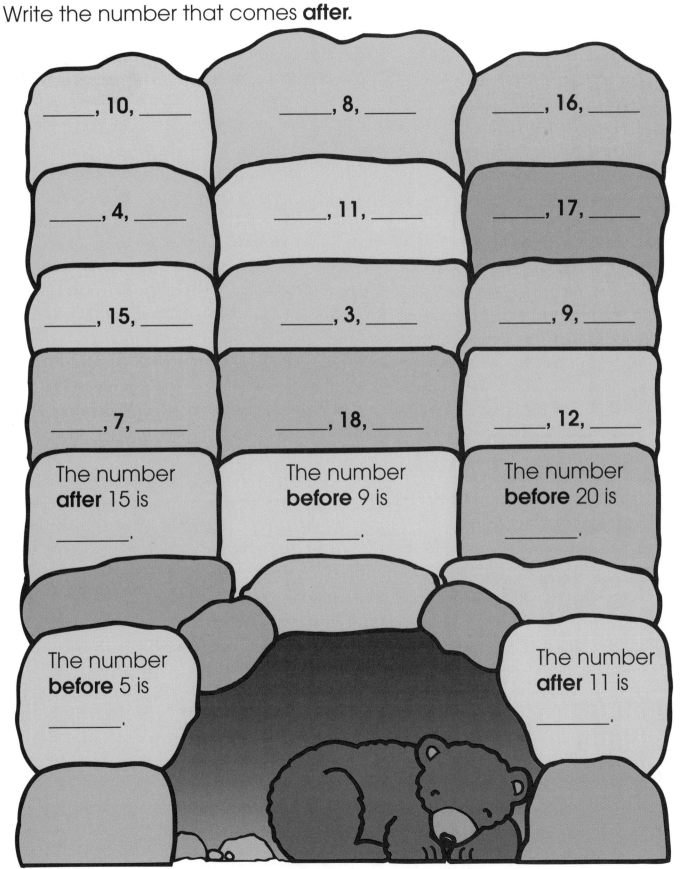

_____ , 10, _____   _____ , 8, _____   _____ , 16, _____

_____ , 4, _____   _____ , 11, _____   _____ , 17, _____

_____ , 15, _____   _____ , 3, _____   _____ , 9, _____

_____ , 7, _____   _____ , 18, _____   _____ , 12, _____

The number **after** 15 is _____ .

The number **before** 9 is _____ .

The number **before** 20 is _____ .

The number **before** 5 is _____ .

The number **after** 11 is _____ .

Cowboy Chow

Write how many tens and ones.
Then write the number.

_____ tens _____ ones = _____

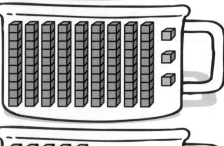

_____ tens _____ ones = _____

_____ tens _____ ones = _____

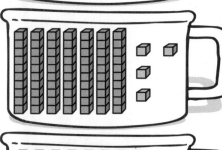

_____ tens _____ ones = _____

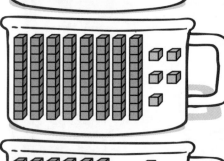

_____ tens _____ ones = _____

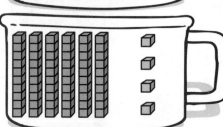

_____ tens _____ ones = _____

At Home: Count out ten zippered plastic bags together. Count out groups of ten pretzel sticks and place ten in each baggie. Have your child use the bags of pretzel sticks and individual pretzels to make the numbers. Chow down!

Name _____

Chili Pepper Place Value

Count the chili peppers. Write the number.

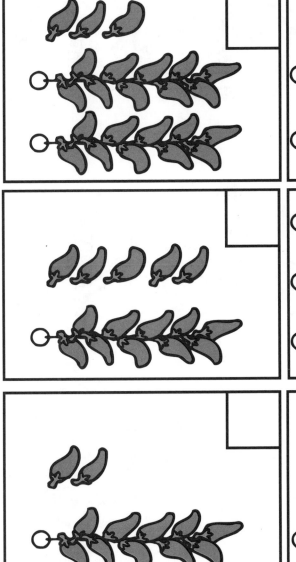

Look at the number.
Draw chili peppers to match.

25

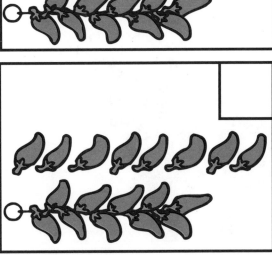

©The Education Center, Inc. • Learning Library® • Math • TEC3717

43

Name _____

Cowpoke Roundup

Count the number of tens and ones.
Write the number.
The first one is done for you.

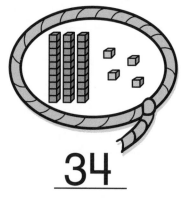
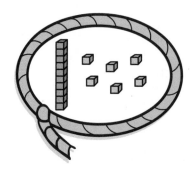
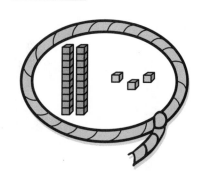

34 _____ _____

_____ _____ _____

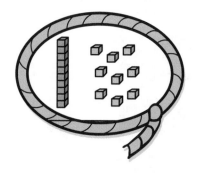
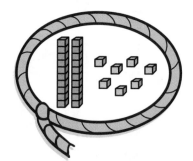
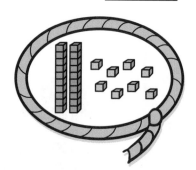

_____ _____ _____

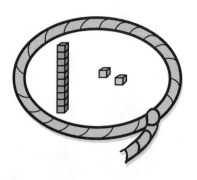

_____

44

©The Education Center, Inc. • *Learning Library*® • *Math* • TEC3717

Name _____

Lasso Larry

Cut and glue each number in order.

41	42		44	45	46	47		49	50
51		53	54		56	57	58	59	
61	62	63		65		67	68		70
	72		74	75	76			79	80
81		83	84		86	87	88	89	
	92	93		95	96	97	98		100

52	69	48	85	64	71	90	78	55
66	73	60	91	77	94	43	99	82

Horseshoe Happenings

Skip-count each pattern.
Write the missing number in the blank.

10 , 20 , ___ , 40 , ___ , 60

2 , 4 , ___ , ___ , 10 , ___

5 , 10 , ___ , ___ , 25 , ___

30 , 35 , ___ , 45 , ___

14 , 16 , 18 , ___ , 22 , ___ , ___

70 , ___ , 90 , ___

Fractions

When your child was a kindergartner, she learned that when she shared one-half of a cookie with a friend, each child received the same or an *equal* portion. In first grade, your child will learn that *one-half* or 1/2 means two equal parts.

First graders should be able to
- share 1/2 of a whole or set
- color 1/2 of a picture set
- recognize that 1/3 and 1/4 mean one out of three or one out of four
- compare fractions such as 1/2 and 1/3 or 1/4
- identify parts of a whole
- use appropriate vocabulary for parts of a whole
- divide sets into equal parts
- solve word problems involving fractions

Equal Parts

Use a candy bar to review equal parts. Purchase at your local store a candy bar that is scored or divided into equal parts, such as a Hershey bar. Ask your child to count how many pieces the bar is divided into. Then ask her to tell you how many pieces she will receive if she shared the bar with you. Provide further practice by having your child tell you how many pieces each person will receive if she shares the candy bar with two or three additional family members.

Key Math Skills for Grade 1
Fractions

- Equal parts and unequal parts
- Identifying parts of a whole: 1/2, 1/3, 1/4
- Identifying parts of a set: 1/2, 1/3, 1/4
- Problem solving with common fractions
- Division: distribution of equal shares

Name _____

Equal Pieces

We can cut **whole** things to make **equal** pieces.

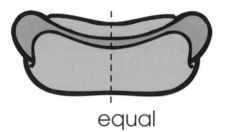

equal   not equal

Color each food that's divided **equally.**

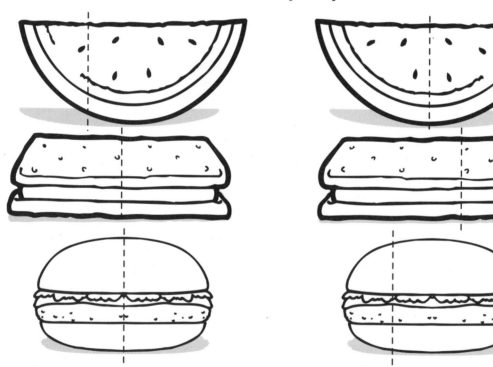

Draw a line to show two **equal** pieces.

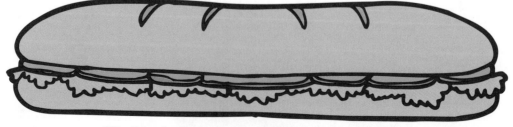

48

Sand Castle Fractions

The flag has two equal parts.

Each part is **one-half.**

We write $\frac{1}{2}$.

Color one-half.

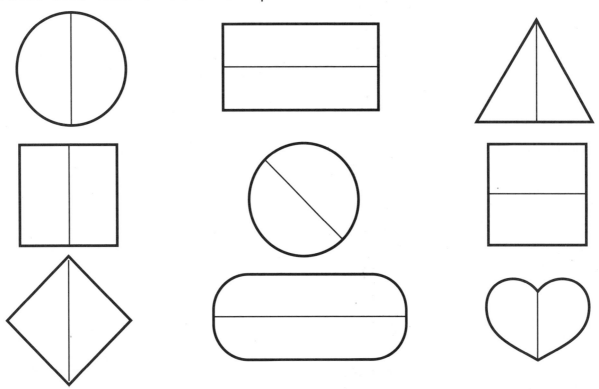

Color **one-half** of each shape.

Beach Towel Pieces

The beach towel has four equal parts.

Each part is **one-fourth.**

We write $\frac{1}{4}$.

Color **one-fourth**.

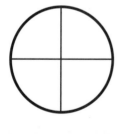  

Color **one-fourth** of each shape.

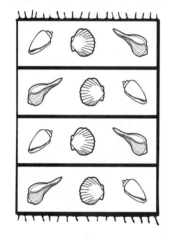 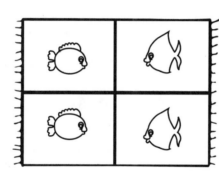 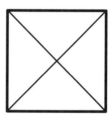

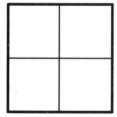 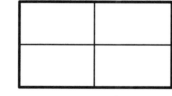 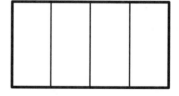

 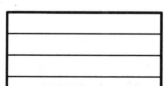 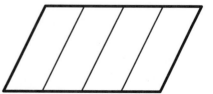

Chocolate Cake Fractions

One-half is shaded.

One-fourth is shaded.

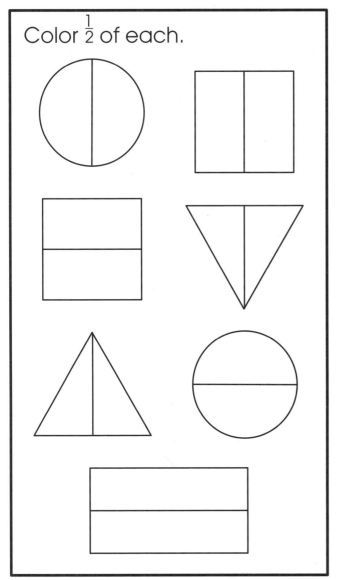

Color $\frac{1}{2}$ of each.

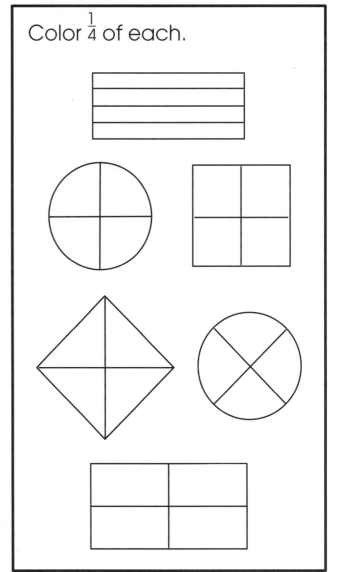

Color $\frac{1}{4}$ of each.

Three Equal Pieces

The cake has **three parts**.
The three parts are **equal**.
Each part is one-third.
We write $\frac{1}{3}$.

Color **one-third** of each cake.

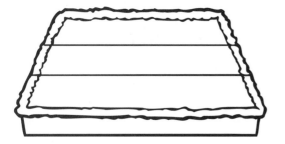  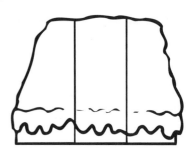

Color **one-third** of each shape.

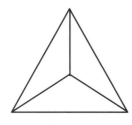 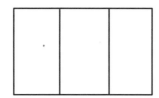 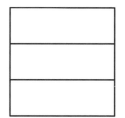

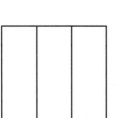  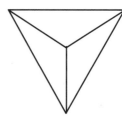

Draw lines on the cake to make
  three equal pieces.
Color **one-third**.

Name_____

Birthday Party Blowout

Look at each set.
Follow the directions for each one.

Circle **one-half** of each set.

  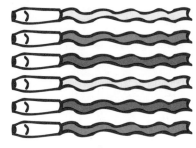

Circle **one-fourth** of each set.

Circle **one-third** of each set.

Name_____

How Many?

Read and solve.

Three friends will share the 9 goody bags. How many will each friend get?	
Liz has 6 cupcakes. She wants to share half of them with her friend Suzi. How many cupcakes will Liz have left?	
Chris has 8 balloons. He wants to share them with his friend Darcy. How many balloons will Chris and Darcy each have?	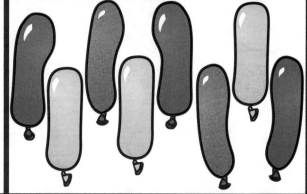
Molly had 3 friends over to play. Molly had 12 dolls for her friends to play with. If each friend had an equal number of dolls, how many dolls did each one get?	

At Home: Pour $1/4$ cup of elbow macaroni onto a surface. Have your child sort the macaroni into as many *equal* groups as she can.

Measurement

Measurement lessons in first grade begin with learning about *nonstandard units.* Your child will learn to measure the length and width of objects using paper clips, pencils, erasers, and blocks. He will learn that these measurements vary depending on size.

First graders should be able to

- use a ruler to measure in inches and *centimeters*

- recognize that a centimeter is smaller than an inch

- know there are 12 inches in a foot

- use a classroom balance to measure weight in nonstandard units such as blocks or counters

- read scales in pounds

- estimate the weight of objects as either more or less than a pound

- recognize that different containers have different capacities

- read a thermometer in degrees Fahrenheit

Key Math Skills for Grade 1
Measurement

Order by size from smallest to biggest

Measuring length: standard and nonstandard units

Measuring length: inches

Measuring length: centimeters

Estimating length: inches

Estimating weight: more or less than a pound

Comparing weights with balances and creates equality

Comparing capacity: more or less than

Reading a thermometer

Choosing the appropriate measuring tool

55

Name_____

A Tall Order

How tall is each stack?
Estimate in paper clips and write.
Measure with paper clips and write.

Estimate.	Estimate.	Estimate.	Estimate.	Estimate.
___ paper clips	___ paper clips	___ paper clips	___ paper clips	___ paper clips
Measure.	Measure.	Measure.	Measure.	Measure.
___ paper clips	___ paper clips	___ paper clips	___ paper clips	___ paper clips

©The Education Center, Inc. • Learning Library® • Math • TEC3717

Flipping Over Measurement

Measure the length of each pan
   from • to •.
Write how many inches.

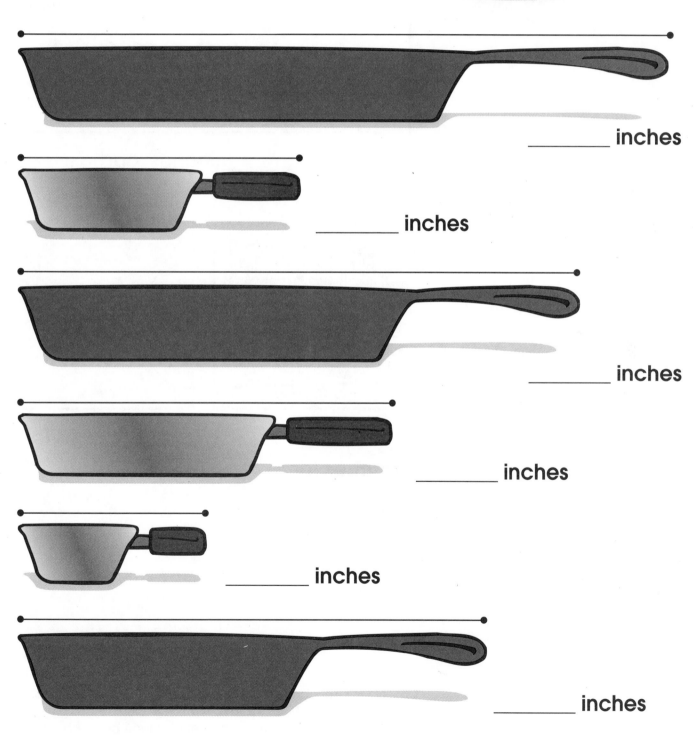

_____ inches

_____ inches

_____ inches

_____ inches

_____ inches

_____ inches

Measure It Yourself

How **long** is each envelope? Measure.
Write the number.

_____ inches long

_____ inches long

_____ inches long

_____ inches long

Draw an envelope. Make it **6 inches long.**

At Home: The mouse near each envelope has a tail that's just as long as the envelope. Cut a piece of yarn the same length as each envelope; then glue each piece beneath its envelope to show how long that mouse's tail is.

Name _____

Help Mr. Groundhog

Measure each object in centimeters.
Write the number above each object.

_____ centimeters

_____ centimeters

_____ centimeters

_____ centimeters

_____ centimeters

_____ centimeters

_____ centimeters

_____ centimeters

Going the Distance

Measure each distance.
Write the number.

_____ centimeters

_____ centimeters

_____ centimeters

_____ centimeters

_____ centimeters

_____ centimeters

_____ centimeters

_____ centimeters

Add to solve.

How far is it from the leaf to the nut? _____ centimeters

How far is it from Phil to the mouse? _____ centimeters

Name _____

Measure My Shadow

How long is each shadow?
Estimate in inches and write.
Measure in inches and write.

Estimate. _____ inches

Measure. _____ inches

Estimate. _____ inches

Measure. _____ inches

Estimate. _____ inches

Measure. _____ inches

Estimate. _____ inches

Measure. _____ inches

Estimate. _____ inches

Measure. _____ inches

Ruler

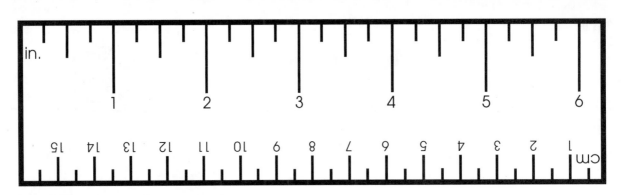

Graph Paper

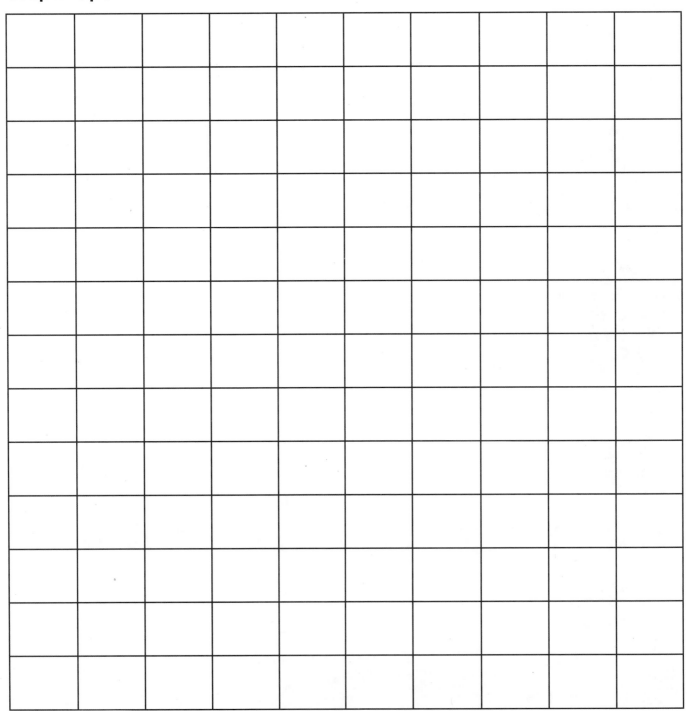

At Home: Cut out and use the ruler as needed with the measurement activities. Use the graph paper on a flat surface to help your child understand area and perimeter. Provide dry beans or cereal and ask your child to cover 4 rows of 4 boxes. Have your child count the total boxes covered to show that an area 4 beans by 4 beans totals 16 beans. Have your child place the 16 beans in a cup. Have your child cover another area that is 5 beans by 5 beans and compare the number of beans needed.

©The Education Center, Inc. • *Learning Library®* • *Math* • TEC3717

What's the Weight?

How much does each bunch of fruit weigh?
Write the number.

_____ pounds   _____ pounds

_____ pounds   _____ pounds

_____ pounds   _____ pounds

Weigh It Yourself

About how much does each package weigh?
Write **more** or **less** for each package.

This is a necklace.

Ms. Rabbit's package
weighs

_____ **than a pound.**

This is dog food.

Dr. Dog's package
weighs

_____ **than a pound.**

This is a t.v.

Baby Bear's package
weighs

_____ **than a pound.**

This is five books.

Mr. Pig's package
weighs

_____ **than a pound.**

This is roller skates.

Miss Kitty's package
weighs

_____ **than a pound.**

This is a hat.

Mrs. Fox's package
weighs

_____ **than a pound.**

Name_____

Cool Containers

Look at each set of containers.
Circle the container that contains **more**.

Capacity means
how much a
container can
hold.

1.

2.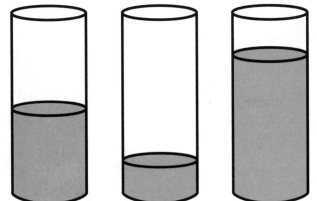

3.

4.

5.

6.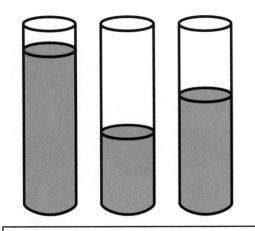

7.

At Home: Pour dry rice into a variety of containers. Have your child tell you which
containers hold *more,* which hold *less,* and which hold *the same.*

Monkey Match

Read each temperature.
Color the thermometer.
Draw a line to match the correct monkey.

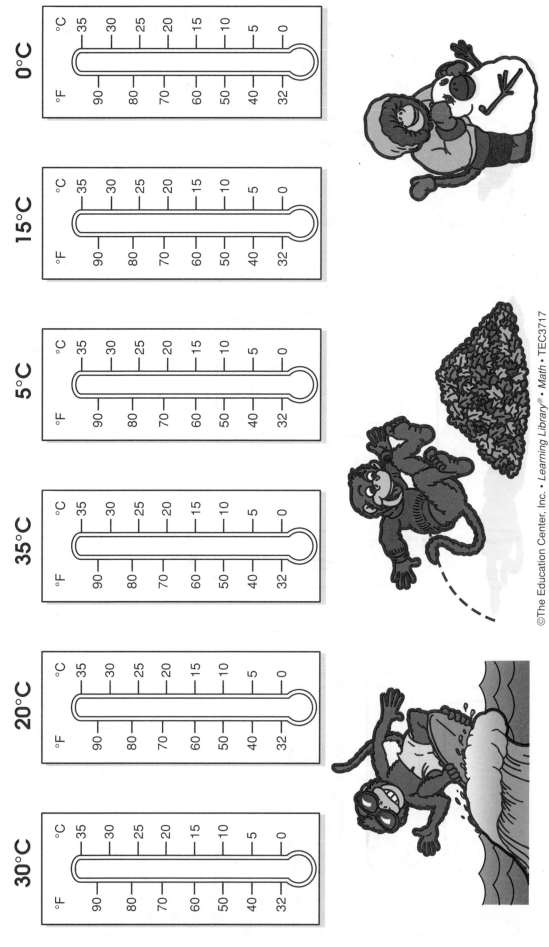

Time and Money

Your child will get daily practice in reading and using a classroom calendar. First graders should be able to use a calendar to
- identify the month, day, and year
- tell the day of the week it is today, what day it was yesterday, and what day tomorrow will be
- identify what day of the week the month begins
- count how many Saturdays the month contains
- identify dates of important events or holidays

First graders begin telling time, first on an *analog clock* and then on a digital clock. Your child should know
- how to write times using the colon to separate the hour from the minutes
- that the smaller hand points to the hour and the larger hand to the minutes
- how to tell time to the hour and the half hour
- how to solve problems involving *elapsed time,* telling how much time has passed

In first grade, your child will practice counting and adding money. First graders can
- identify different coins and their values: *penny, nickel, dime, quarter,* and *half-dollar*
- count coin combinations up to 50 cents, starting with the coin with the greatest value
- solve problems involving money

Key Math Skills for Grade 1
Time and Money

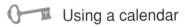

- Using a calendar
- Reading analog and digital clocks
- Time to the hour
- Time to the half hour
- Time to the quarter hour
- Identifying events before or after a given time
- Word problems with time
- Identifying coins and sets of coins to 50 cents
- Counting coin combinations to 50 cents
- Word problems with money to 50 cents

December Days

Look at the calendar.
Answer these questions by writing a day of the week.

1. The first day of this month is on _____ .

2. The last day of this month is on _____ .

3. The day after Thursday is _____ .

Answer each question by matching it with a number.

1. How many days are in the month?   16

2. How many Thursdays are in the month?   31

3. What date is Dan's birthday?   5

4. What was the date when it began to snow?   4

5. What was the first sunny date in the month?   22

Draw in the box to show what the weather was like on each of these days.

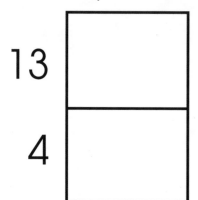

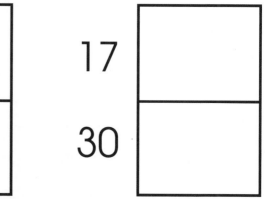

December

Sunday	Monday	Tuesday	Wednesday	Thursday	Friday	Saturday
This calendar belongs to:				1	2	3
4	5	6	7	8	9	10
11	12	13	14	15	16 Happy Birthday, Dan!	17
18	19	20	21	22	23	24
25	26	27	28	29	30	31

Sleeping the Hours Away

Write each time.

____ : ____   ____ : ____   ____ : ____   ____ : ____

____ : ____   ____ : ____   ____ : ____   ____ : ____

Draw hands to show each time.

__7__ : __00__   __6__ : __00__   __3__ : __00__   __11__ : __00__

Try This:
What time do you go to bed? Color the clock above that reads closest to that time.

SNORE

Time Ticks By

Write each time.

____ : ____   ____ : ____   ____ : ____   ____ : ____

____ : ____   ____ : ____   ____ : ____   ____ : ____

Draw hands to show each time.

__8__ : __30__   __9__ : __30__   __12__ : __30__   __3__ : __30__

Try This:
Color the clock above that reads one half hour before 3:00.

Wake Up, Bear!

Write each time.

_____ : _____   _____ : _____   _____ : _____   _____ : _____

_____ : _____   _____ : _____   _____ : _____   _____ : _____

Draw hands to show each time.

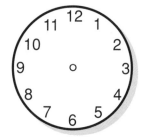   

___7___ : _30_   ___1___ : _30_   __10__ : _30_   ___4___ : _30_

Try This:
What time do you wake up? Color the clock above that reads nearest that time.

Time to Get Going!

Write each time.

____ : ____   ____ : ____   ____ : ____   ____ : ____

____ : ____   ____ : ____   ____ : ____   ____ : ____

Draw hands to show each time.

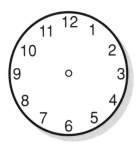   

__11__ : __30__   __8__ : __00__   __3__ : __00__   __6__ : __30__

Try This:
What time do you eat breakfast? Color the clock above that reads nearest that time.

Time: Problem solving

Time to Tell

Read each problem.
Write the time on the line.
Draw the hands on the clock to match.

---

1. Billy Bear started eating his honey at 9:00. It took him 30 minutes to eat. What time did Billy finish?

_ _ : _ _

2. At 7:00 this morning, the rooster started to crow. He crowed for 1 hour. What time did he stop?

_ _ : _ _

3. It was 11:00 when Betty Bear went out for a walk. She walked for 30 minutes. What time did Betty return?

_ _ : _ _

---

4. Baby Bear started to rake the lawn at 3:30. He was finished in a half hour. What time did he finish?

_ _ : _ _

5. Today is Billy's day to clean the den. It will take him 30 minutes. If he starts at 2:00, what time will he be done?

_ _ : _ _

6. Betty Bear is going to visit Rick Raccoon. It is a 30-minute walk to his house. It is 4:00 now. What time will Betty get there?

_ _ : _ _

---

7. Mama Bear needs to cook dinner. She will start at 5:30. It will take her one hour. What time will she be done?

_ _ : _ _

8. Papa Bear reads a bedtime story to Baby Bear each night. He will start at 7:00. It will take 30 minutes. When will Papa Bear be finished?

_ _ : _ _

9. Bedtime is almost here! It is 7:30. Baby Bear must go to bed in 30 minutes. What time will Baby Bear go to bed?

_ _ : _ _

Dolphin Discovery

How much? Circle the cents.

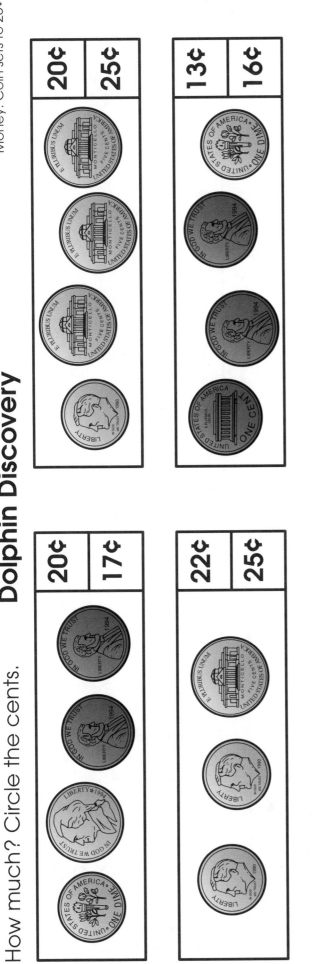

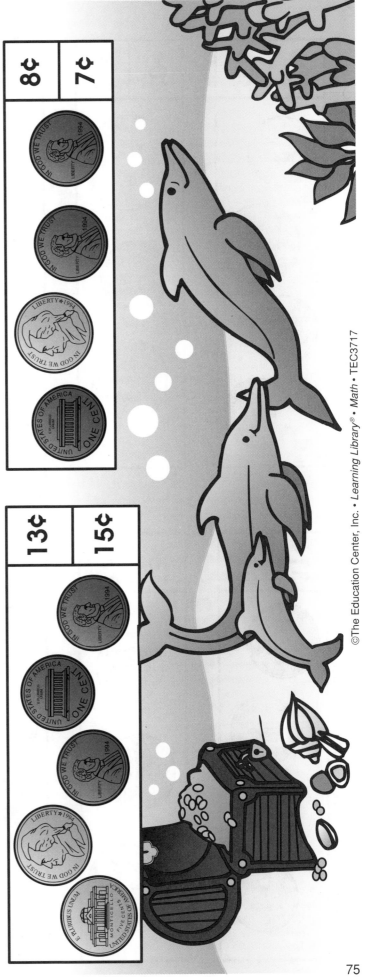

Treasure in My Arms

How much? Circle the cents.

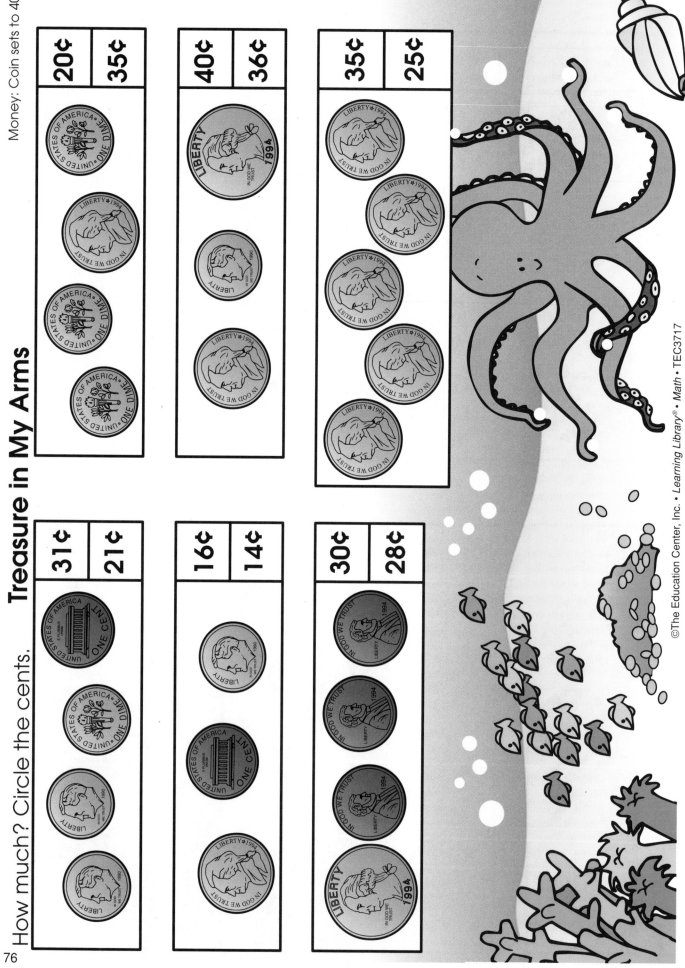

20¢
35¢

40¢
36¢

35¢
25¢

31¢
21¢

16¢
14¢

30¢
28¢

A Clawful of Coins

How much? Circle the cents.

38¢	40¢
28¢	14¢

50¢	32¢
45¢	37¢

25¢	50¢
50¢	46¢

Name _____

Money: Counting coins to 25¢

Shoppin' Shirley

Help Shirley fill her basket with toys.
Color the coins to show how much.

1. 17¢

2. 9¢

3. 12¢

4. 10¢

5. 21¢

6. 24¢

7. 18¢

8. 7¢

9. 15¢

At Home: Provide your child with a supply of clipped coupons and a variety of coin amounts. Have him count out change to equal the cents off on each coupon.

78

©The Education Center, Inc. • *Learning Library*® • *Math* • TEC3717

Name _____

Junk Food Jimmy

Count the coins.
Write how much.

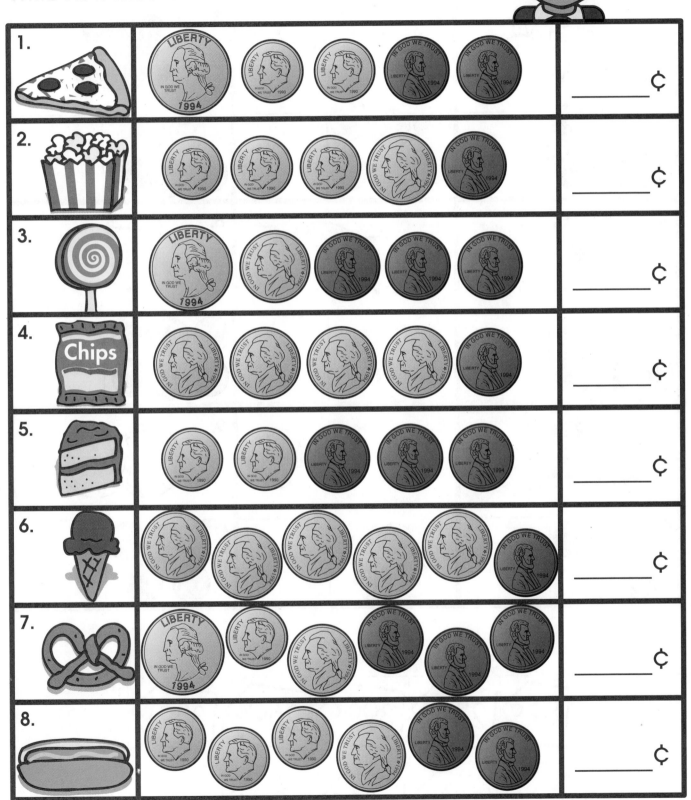

Name_____

Money Magic

Count the coins.
Cut and paste each matching tag.

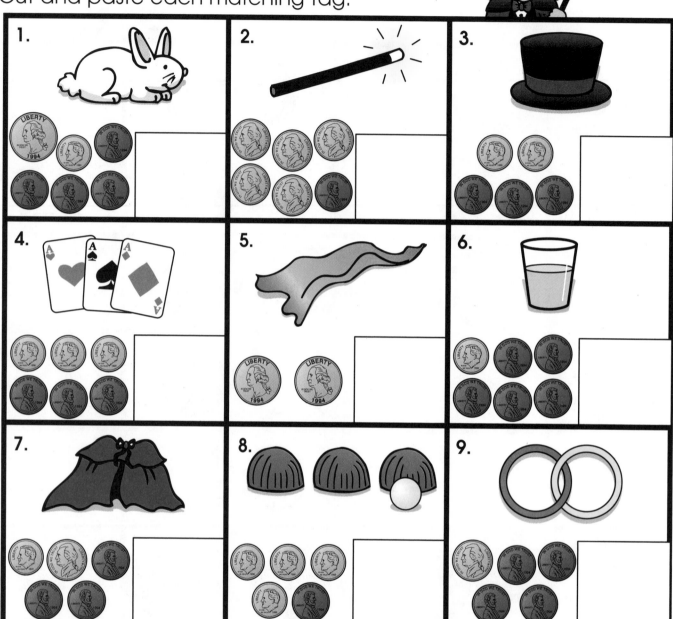

Name _____

Let's Shop!

Read each problem.
Count the money.
Write how much.

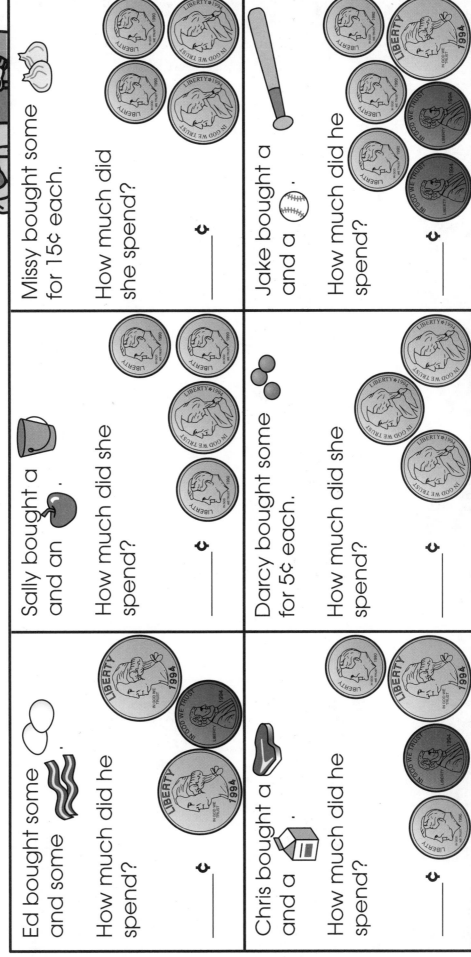

Ed bought some ⬡⬡ and some 〰️ .

How much did he spend?

¢ _____

Sally bought a 🪣 and an 🍎 .

How much did she spend?

¢ _____

Missy bought some 🐚 for 15¢ each.

How much did she spend?

¢ _____

Chris bought a ⬟ and a 🏠 .

How much did he spend?

¢ _____

Darcy bought some ● for 5¢ each.

How much did she spend?

¢ _____

Jake bought a 🏏 and a ⚾ .

How much did he spend?

¢ _____

At Home: Go on a shopping spree right in your kitchen! Have your little one "purchase" items using spare change. Have him count out his money as he "pays" for each item.

Geometry

First graders learn to identify and name two-dimensional shapes such as *triangles, squares, circles, rectangles, hexagons, diamonds,* and *trapezoids.* They also learn the names of three-dimensional shapes such as *cone, cube, sphere,* and *rectangular solid.* They begin to understand that different shapes have different numbers of sides and corners.

In first grade, your child will learn how to

- identify characteristics of *plane* (two-dimensional) and *solid* (three-dimensional) geometric shapes

- sort plane figures by size, color, shape, number of sides or corners

- make *symmetrical* shapes by cutting and folding paper, using mirrors, or painting

- identify *transformations* (made by flipping, sliding, or turning shapes)

- use position words such as *in front of, behind, left of, right of, over, and under*

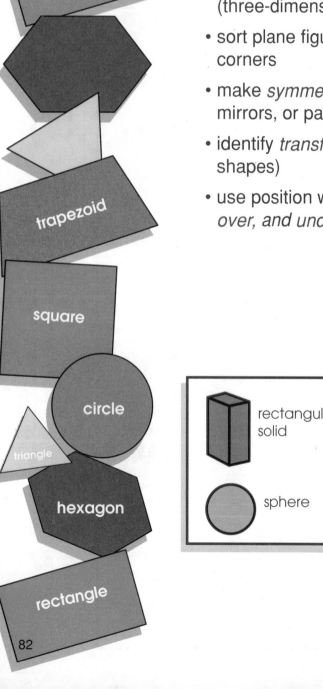

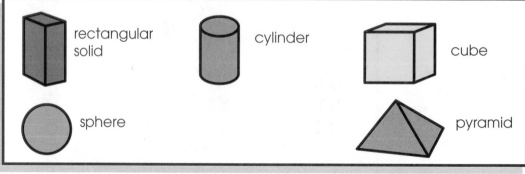

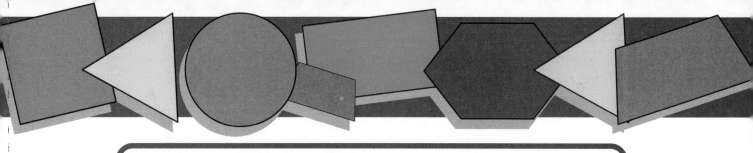

Key Math Skills for Grade 1
Geometry

O─ᴨ Plane shapes: identifying rectangles, triangles, squares, circles

O─ᴨ Plane shapes: counting the number of sides and corners

O─ᴨ Solid shapes: recognizing cylinders, cubes, spheres, prisms, rectangular solids

O─ᴨ Position and direction words: in front of, behind, left of, right of, over, and under

O─ᴨ Identifying symmetry

O─ᴨ Recognizing shapes from different perspectives

O─ᴨ Recognizing geometric shapes and structures in the environment

Left Or Right?

Next time you're riding in the car with your child for an appointment or another trip, pose different proximity questions using objects you see from the car windows. Ask your child questions such as the following: Is the tree to the *left* or *right* of the mailbox? Is McDonald's to the *left* or *right* of K-Mart? Is the bird at the *top* or the *bottom* of the tree? Is the bridge *over* or *under* the road? Then challenge your child to come up with his own questions for you to answer.

Symmetry Paintings

Practice creating symmetrical objects by painting them! Cover a workspace with newspaper. Provide your child with a variety of paints or fingerpaints. Then fold a large sheet of white paper in half. Instruct your child to paint or fingerpaint a design on one-half of the paper. Then direct him to fold his paper in half, pressing the wet painted side to the unpainted one. Unfold the paper to allow your child to discover his own symmetrical painting!

For even more symmetry practice, have your child fold a sheet of construction paper in half. Direct him to draw a design along the fold of the paper and cut around the design. Have him unfold his paper to see what symmetrical design he has created.

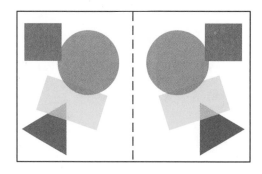

Shape Scene

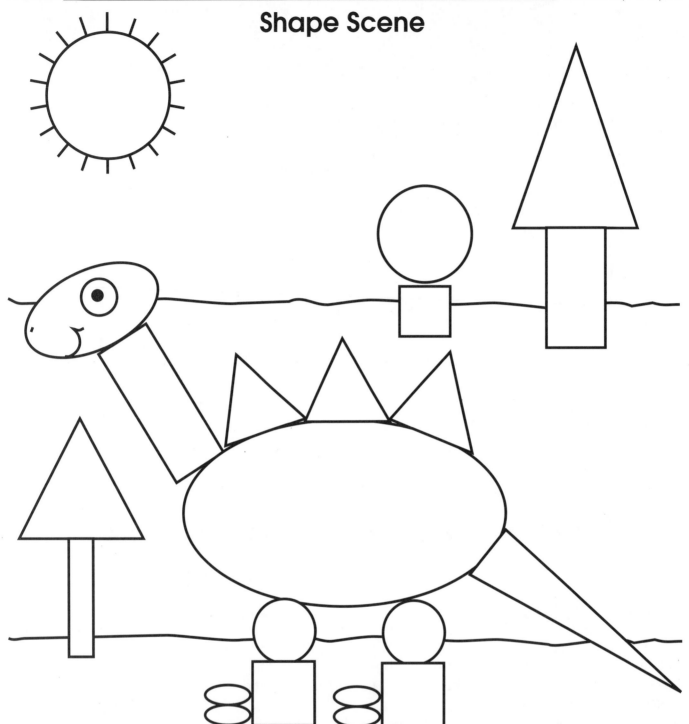

Color by the code.

 yellow   orange   green

red   brown

Searching for Shapes

Count the number of each shape.
Write how many.

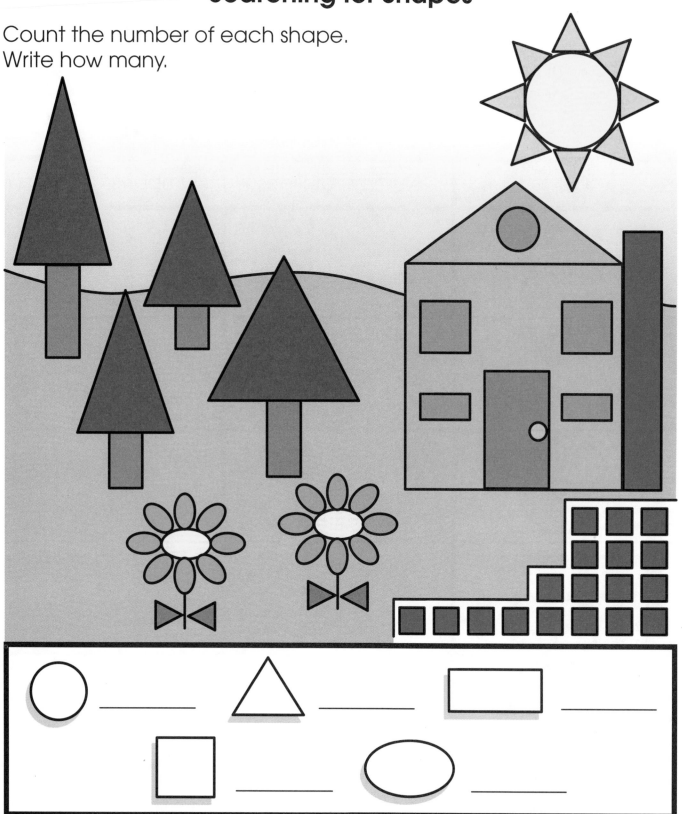

Name _____

Shape-O

Look at each figure.
Write how many **sides**.
Write how many **corners**.

Shape	Number of Sides	Number of Corners

Name _____

3-D Robot

Color by the code.

red

green

yellow

orange

blue

At Home: Have your child give the names for three-dimensional objects around the house, such as cereal boxes, soup cans, balls, and blocks. Ask, "Why do balls roll in a straight line, but cones roll to one side?"

Dreamy Dragon

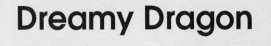

 The ◯ is on the **top**.

 The ▢ is on the **bottom**.

Color the **top** shapes **yellow**.

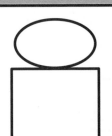   

Now color the **bottom** shapes **blue**.

The ◯ is on the **left.**

The ☐ is on the **right.**

Color the shapes on the **left red.**

My Favorite Dragon

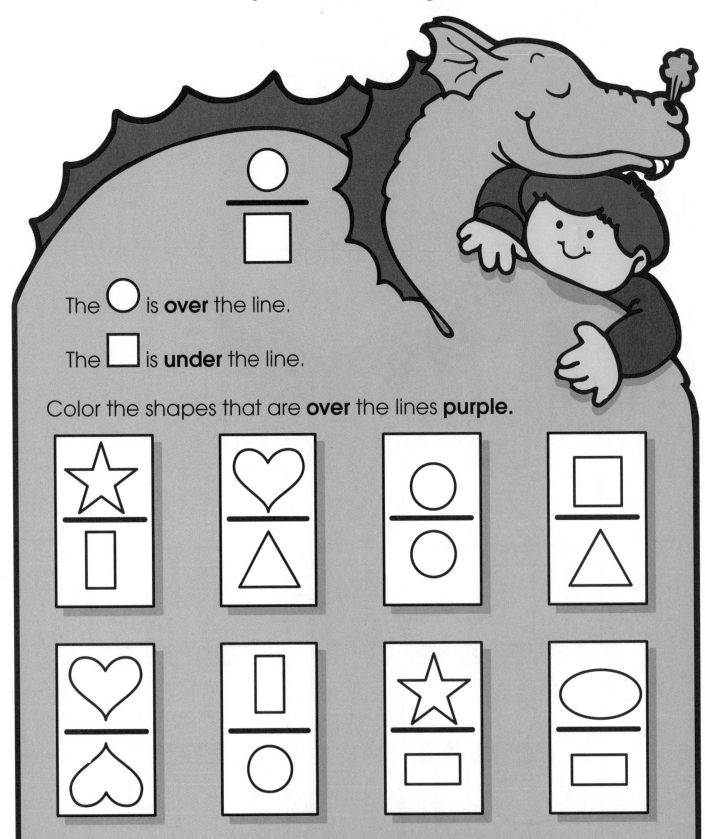

The ◯ is **over** the line.

The ☐ is **under** the line.

Color the shapes that are **over** the lines **purple.**

Now color the shapes that are **under** the lines **yellow.**

Name _____

Just Flippin' Around

Write **flip** or **turn** on each line.

1. 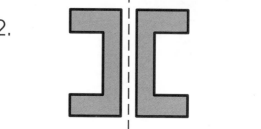 _____

2. 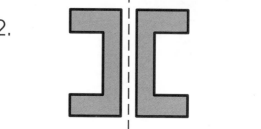 _____

3. 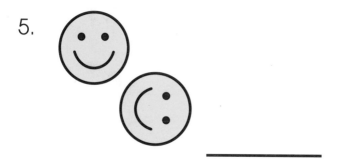 _____

4. 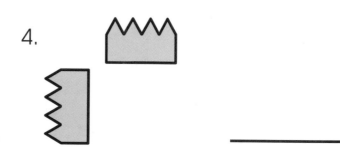 _____

5. 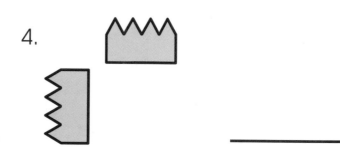 _____

6. 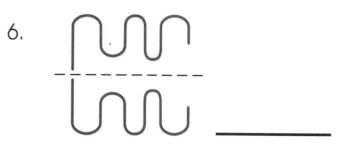 _____

7. 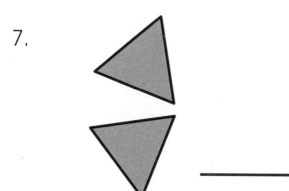 _____

8. 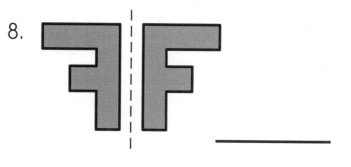 _____

Name _____

Geometry Workout

Circle the word.

 The s are **over/under** the .

The is on the **top/bottom** of the

 The is to the **left/right** of the

The is **over/under** the .

 The is to the **left/right** of the .

Color by the code.

 and red   and green

and blue   and yellow

Patterns, Functions, and Algebra

Your child will learn how patterns, functions, and algebra play an important role in the world around her. Yes, there's *algebra* in first grade! But don't worry. It's not the algebra that stumped you in high school. Your child will learn

- many things change over time, many changes are predictable
- changes can be represented using symbols and equations

Even first graders can begin to use math models to understand how a change in one variable affects the output or result. First graders can draw pictures and use manipulatives to

- find the missing *addends* in problems (5 + __ = 9)
- model addition and subtraction problems
- complete charts that show a *function,* such as adding 4
- write number sentences with symbols such as +, −

Sorting and classifying objects are concepts most first graders find quite simple. First graders can

- sort, classify, and order objects by size
- sort objects by shape, number, or other properties
- recognize and extend patterns such as sequences of shapes or simple numbers
- skip-count by twos, threes, fives, and tens
- skip-count to 100 using a hundreds chart (If you count by tens beginning with 36, what number would you color next?)

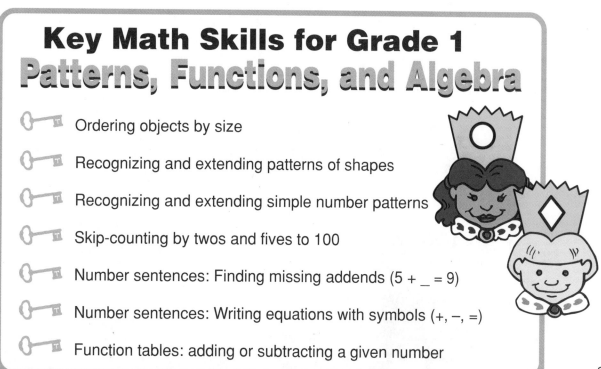

Key Math Skills for Grade 1
Patterns, Functions, and Algebra

- Ordering objects by size
- Recognizing and extending patterns of shapes
- Recognizing and extending simple number patterns
- Skip-counting by twos and fives to 100
- Number sentences: Finding missing addends (5 + _ = 9)
- Number sentences: Writing equations with symbols (+, −, =)
- Function tables: adding or subtracting a given number

Name _____

Just Right!

Help the Bear Family.
Cut and paste each set from smallest to biggest.

Baby Bear   Mama Bear   Papa Bear

At Home: Read the tale of The Three Bears with your child. Leave out the repeating phrase and ask, "What comes next?" After reading, ask your child to name other personal items that Goldilocks might have seen in the Bears' home. Do the bears have spoons, shoes, coats, and bicycles in different sizes? Have her draw these items from largest to smallest.

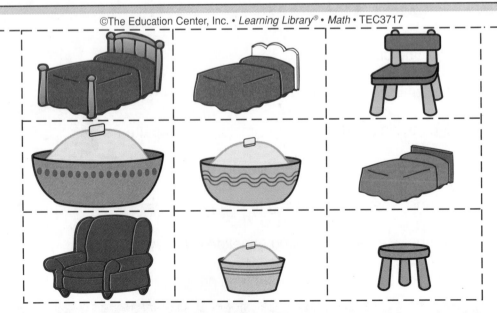

Name_____

Pick a Pumpkin Pattern

Finish each pattern.

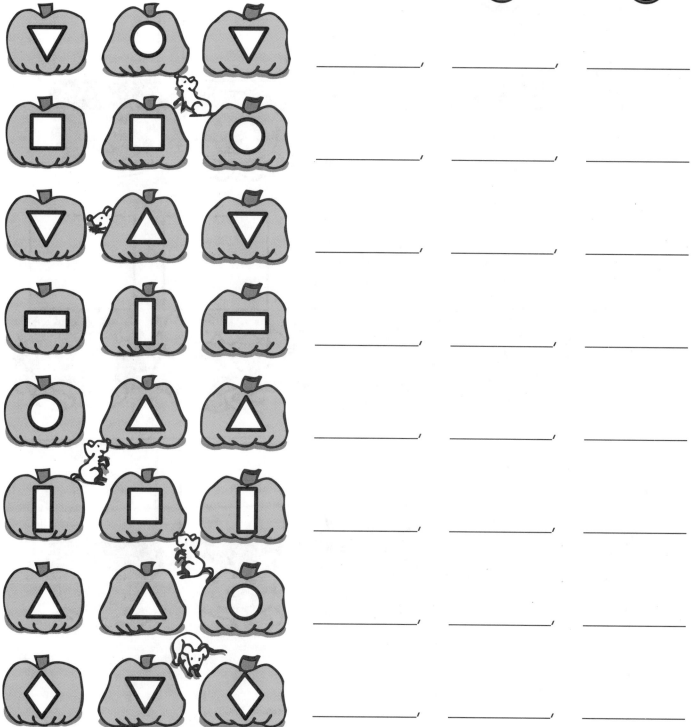

_____ , _____ , _____

_____ , _____ , _____

_____ , _____ , _____

_____ , _____ , _____

_____ , _____ , _____

_____ , _____ , _____

_____ , _____ , _____

_____ , _____ , _____

At Home: Using colored toothpicks, make simple repeating color or number patterns. Ask, "How can this pattern be repeated or extended?" Explain ways to get to the next element in the pattern.

Royal Family Fun

Finish each pattern.
Cut and paste the crowns.

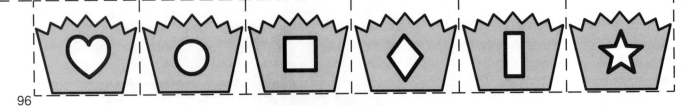

Name_____

Miss Fairy's Mix-Up

Help Miss Fairy correct each pattern.
Write the numbers on the lines.

10 5 20 15	____, ____, ____, ____
4 2 8 6	____, ____, ____, ____
7 3 5 9	____, ____, ____, ____
20 10 30 40	____, ____, ____, ____
45 35 30 40	____, ____, ____, ____
12 16 14 18	____, ____, ____, ____

Hansel's Sweet Treats

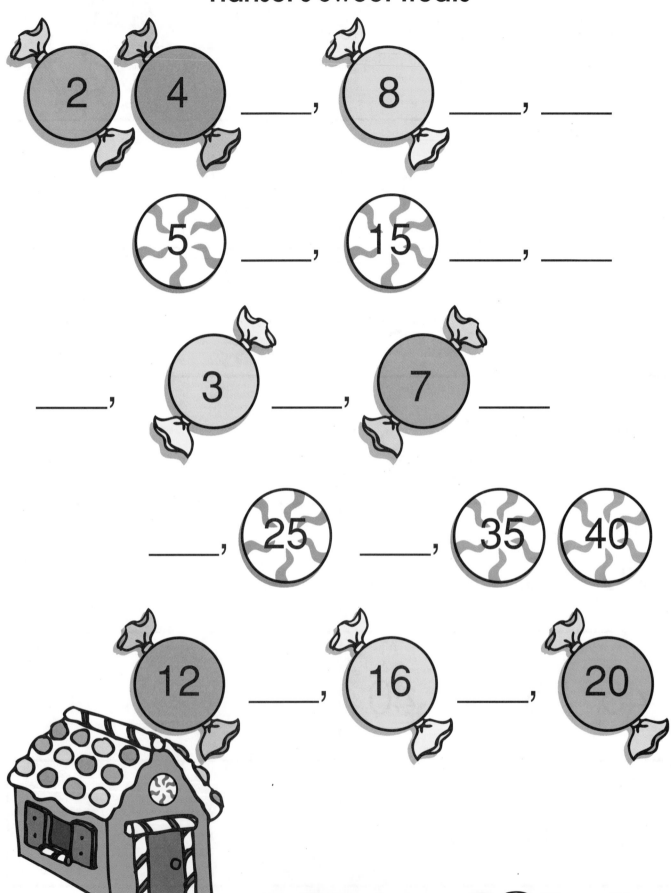

2 4 ____, 8 ____, ____

5 ____, 15 ____, ____

____, 3 ____, 7 ____

____, 25 ____, 35 40

12 ____, 16 ____, 20

Flapjack Stacks

Each pancake costs 2¢. Count each stack by twos. Write the cost of each pancake stack.

Each pancake costs 5¢. Count each stack by fives. Write the cost of each pancake stack.

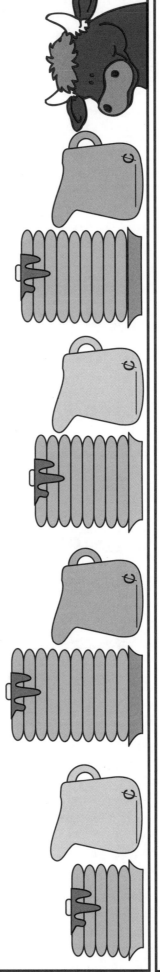

Each pancake costs 10¢. Count each stack by tens. Write the cost of each pancake stack.

Name_____

The Princess and the Peas

Write the missing numbers.

 $5 + \underline{\quad} = 7$

 $\underline{\quad} + 1 = 6$

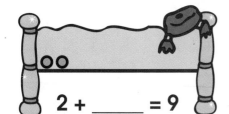 $2 + \underline{\quad} = 9$

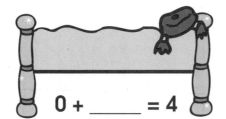 $0 + \underline{\quad} = 4$

$8 + \underline{\quad} = 8$

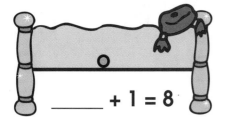 $\underline{\quad} + 1 = 8$

 $3 + \underline{\quad} = 7$

 $10 + \underline{\quad} = 10$

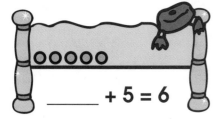 $\underline{\quad} + 5 = 6$

 $5 + \underline{\quad} = 10$

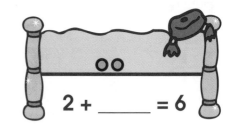 $2 + \underline{\quad} = 6$

 $4 + \underline{\quad} = 5$

 $9 + \underline{\quad} = 9$

 $\underline{\quad} + 4 = 9$

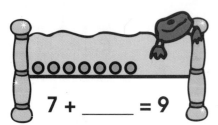 $7 + \underline{\quad} = 9$

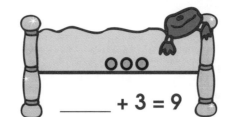 $\underline{\quad} + 3 = 9$

 $2 + \underline{\quad} = 4$

At Home: Make sets similar to those above, using dried peas or beans. Have your child name the number that completes the problem.

Name _____

Tall Towers

Add or subtract.
Write the answer.
The first one has been done for you.

+ 10

6	16
3	13
2	12

– 4

10	
8	
12	

– 3

4	
7	
6	

+ 7

6	
5	
9	

– 1

8	
10	
3	

+ 5

10	
7	
4	

– 2

6	
9	
10	

+ 4

7	
6	
1	

101

Graphing and Probability

Your first grader will learn how to gather information (data) to answer questions about himself and those around him. In school, the teacher will pose questions such as "How many children like chocolate ice cream? How many more children like dogs than cats? Which pet is owned by the fewest children?" He'll survey his classmates and make a tally mark for each response.

Your child will learn the differences between *tallies, pictographs, bar graphs, circle graphs,* and *line graphs* and to choose the best way to present his information.

First graders also learn basic concepts of probability through games such as tossing a coin and marking tallies for the number of heads or tails thrown, tossing dice, or using spinners to find the chances of a color or number. He'll be able to tell whether an outcome has a likely or unlikely chance of occurring and whether an event is certain or impossible.

First graders learn how to
- organize and represent information using objects, pictures, and graphs
- create tallies, picture graphs, and bar graphs
- determine if an outcome is likely or unlikely, certain or impossible

Family Graph

Create a family graph. Enlist the help of your child to choose a desired topic for his survey, such as favorite ice-cream flavors or pets. Have your child ask each family member, including those who do not live in your home, the survey question. Have him make a tally mark for each answer given.

Next, assist your child in creating a graph of his choice on a piece of poster board, using the data he gathered. Help your child include all the necessary parts on the graph: *title, labels,* and *numbers of boxes needed.* Then challenge your youngster to write simple graph-related questions for other family members to solve.

Key Math Skills for Grade 1
Graphing and Probability

- Gathering data: surveys, counts, and tallies
- Sorting and organizing data
- Graphing: pictographs
- Graphing: bar graphs
- Probability: certain or impossible events
- Probability: likely or unlikely events
- Probability: chances of events

In the Bag!

Understanding probability is easy with this fun idea! Fill an empty lunch sack with ten blocks in three different colors. Ask your child to guess which color block will be picked most often from the bag. Then have your child randomly select blocks from the bag, one at a time. Instruct him to mark a tally for each color block selected. Continue until your child has made ten selections. Then have him count the number of tallies for each color. Ask him if his prediction was correct; then empty the bag of blocks so that he may determine why his prediction was correct or incorrect.

Let's Take a Vote!

Next time you're planning a family trip or vacation, have your child set up "choice" bowls. Have your child label a different bowl for each desired trip. Then have him give each family member a different counter. Have each family member choose a trip, over a period of a few days, by dropping a counter into one of the bowls. When the choices have been made, have your child tally up the number of counters in each bowl to determine the location of your family trip!

Pop! Pop! Pop!

Count each kind of balloon.
Draw a tally for each one.

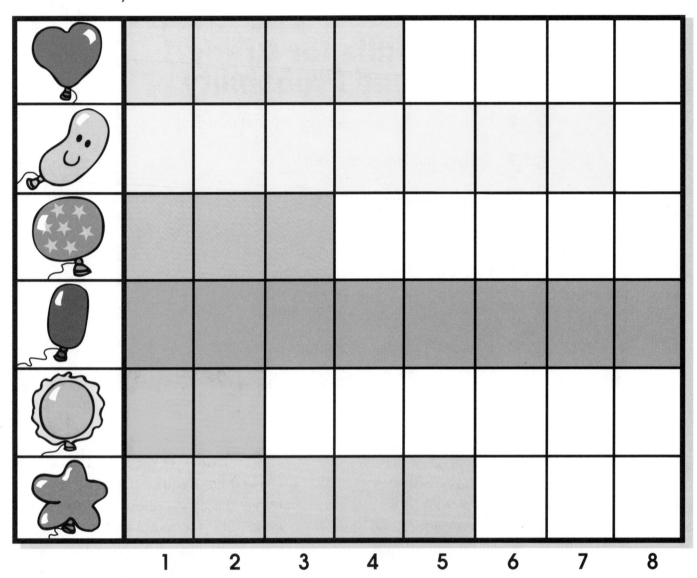

How many?

IIII					

Name_____

Class Pets

Complete the graph.

Draw one  for each animal in the bank.

Pets Bank	
dogs	4
turtles	6
cats	5
fish	3
birds	1
rabbits	2

Class Pets

Dogs						
Turtles						
Cats						
Fish						
Birds						
Rabbits						

A Penguin's Prey

Color one box on the graph for each animal you find in the picture.

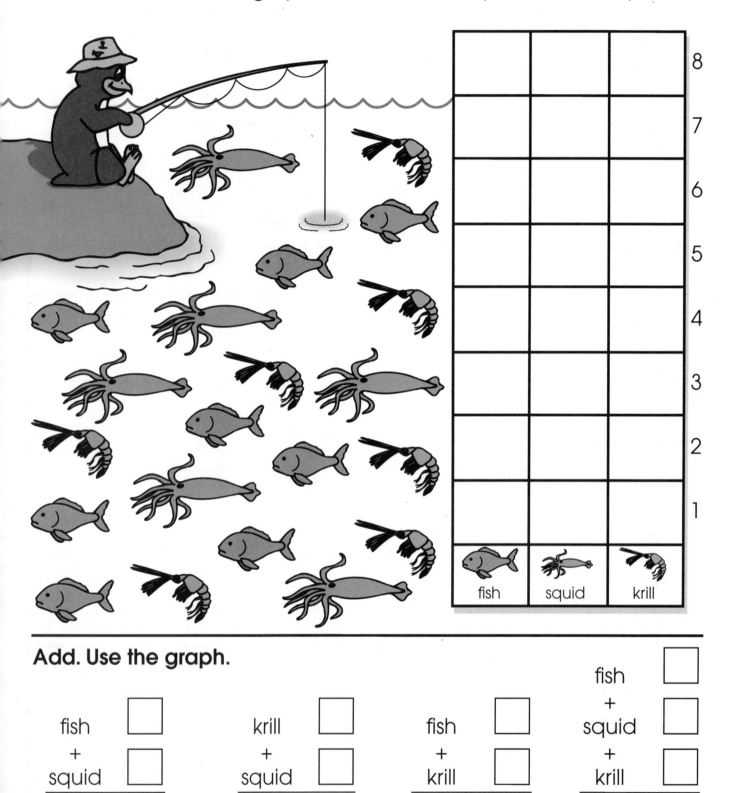

			8
			7
			6
			5
			4
			3
			2
			1
fish	squid	krill

Add. Use the graph.

fish
+
squid
____

krill
+
squid
____

fish
+
krill
____

fish
+
squid
+
krill
____

Name _____

A Graph of Goodies

Color.
Count the jelly beans. Write the totals.
Finish the graph.

Totals	
red	
yellow	
green	
orange	
blue	

7					
6					
5					
4					
3					
2					
1					
	red	yellow	green	orange	blue

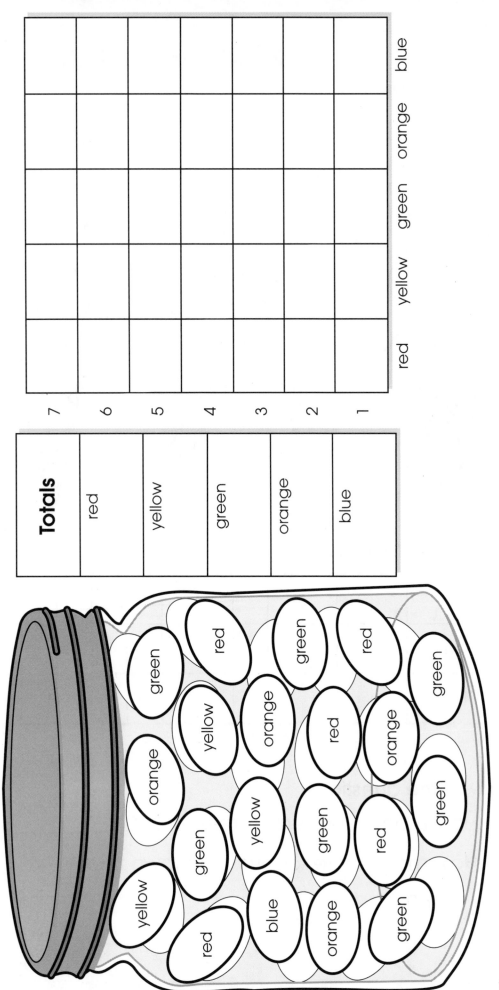

Triple-Scoop Delight

Color.

	green	brown	pink	brown	brown
	pink	brown	brown	green	pink
	brown	green	pink	pink	brown

Complete the graph.

	1	2	3	4	5	6	7	8	9	10	11	12	13	14	15	16
green																
brown																
pink																

Answer the questions.

1. How many scoops are green *or* pink? _____

2. How many *more* scoops are brown than green? _____

Hangin' Around

Color the groups of pictures **yellow** that you are **certain** to find on the wall.
Color the groups of pictures **orange** that are **impossible** to find on the wall.

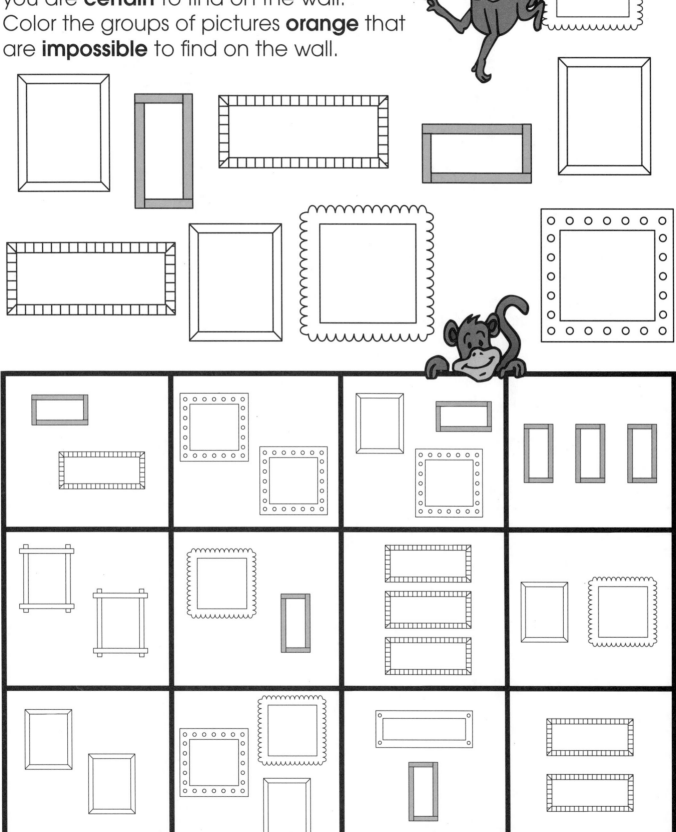

It's in the Bag!

Color the cubes.
Circle the bag you think has more chance of having a yellow block picked.

Bag A

red   yellow   blue
yellow   blue   blue   red
blue   blue   red

Bag B

red   yellow   red
yellow   red   yellow   blue
yellow   yellow   blue

Count the cubes.
Make a tally for each one.

Bag A

Color	Tally Marks
red	
blue	
yellow	

Bag B

Color	Tally Marks
red	
blue	
yellow	

Answer the questions.

Which bag has more yellow cubes? _____

Which bag has fewer yellow cubes? _____

Was your guess right? _____

Problem Solving

Problem solving is woven into all strands of math, from number sense and measurement to geometry and probability. Your first grader will discover there are several different strategies, such as drawing a picture or estimating, that will help her solve different kinds of problems.

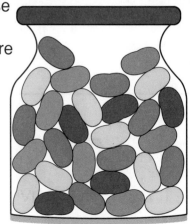

Your child will learn these strategies and develop her own preferred ways to approach problems:

- logical thinking or using clues to eliminate choices
- drawing a picture
- making a list
- acting it out
- estimating the answer

Your youngster should learn there is no one right way to arrive at a solution.

You can help your child develop a positive attitude toward problem solving by modeling mathematical thinking—by asking "out loud" the questions you are thinking as you find math solutions or make decisions. Show your first grader how math helped you decide which item to buy, when to put gas in the car, or when to leave home to pick her up after soccer practice.

Key Math Skills for Grade 1
Problem Solving

- Drawing pictures
- Making a list
- Making a guess
- Estimating tens, ones, and hundreds
- Using logic
- Finding a pattern
- Acting out the problem

It's a Pizza Party!

Read the clues.
Circle the special slice.

It has .

It does not have .

It does not have .

It has .

It has ◎.

It has .

It has .

It has .

At Home: Have your child draw three kinds of pizza with two toppings each. Then pick a pizza and give two clues of your choice.

Name _____

Helmet Hunt

Read the clues.
Color the correct helmets.

1. It has stripes.
   It is not first.
   Which helmet is it?
   Color it blue.

2. It has stars.
   It is not second.
   Which helmet is it?
   Color it yellow.

3. It has stripes.
   It has only one star.
   Which helmet is it?
   Color it green.

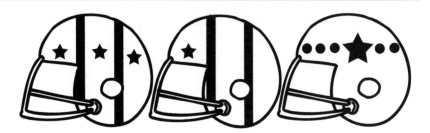

4. It does not have a number.
   It does not have a letter.
   Which helmet is it?
   Color it red.

5. It has two stripes.
   It has a number.
   Which helmet is it?
   Color it purple.

Name _____

Picture This

Draw a picture to help you solve each problem.

Sam has 2 gumballs. Ted gave him 2 more. How many does he have now?	Emily had 5 flowers. She gave 3 of them to Sarah. How many flowers are left?
Chris has 3 goldfish. Mark has 4 goldfish. How many goldfish in all?	Missy found 6 rocks. Darcy found 3 rocks. How many rocks in all?
Jake got 2 balloons at the fair. Carly got 6 balloons at the fair. How many balloons in all?	Amy gave Mike 4 balls. She had 10 to begin with. How many balls does Amy have left?

Name _____

Looking at Legs

Read each problem.
Draw and color a picture of the problem.
Circle the correct answer.

1. There are 2 robins in a tree. How many legs?	2. There are 3 squirrels eating nuts. How many legs?

| 6   4   2 | 12   16   10 |

3. There are 2 deer walking in the woods. How many legs?	4. A spider crawls on a leaf. How many legs?

| 12   10   8 | 6   8   4 |

5. There are 2 robins and 2 deer. Which have fewer legs?	6. There are 2 robins and 1 spider. Which has more legs?

| the robins   the deer | the spider   the robins |

Name _____

Make a Guess

Estimate how many gumballs are
  in each bank.
Then color the gumballs and write
  how many.

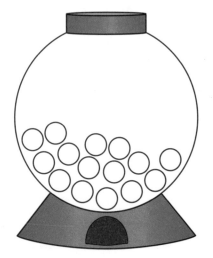

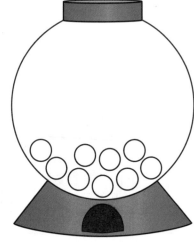

An **estimate** is a
guess that is
neither right nor
wrong.

estimate: _____

actual: _____

estimate: _____

actual: _____

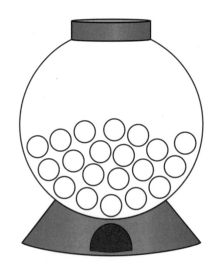

estimate: _____

actual: _____

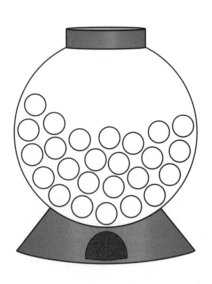

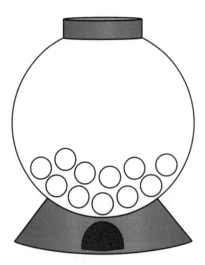

estimate: _____

actual: _____

estimate: _____

actual: _____

Hiking Home

Finish each pattern.

A. 2 4 6 ___ ___ ___ 18

B. 5 10 15 ___ ___ ___ 45

C. 10 20 30 ___ ___ ___ 90

D. 3 6 9 ___ ___ ___ 27

E. A C E ___ ___ ___ Q

Campfire Clues

Color and cut out the marshmallows below.
Use the marshmallows to find the answers.
Write each answer.
Color the marshmallows.

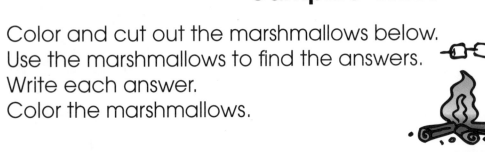

1. Green is first. White is between orange and green. Yellow is next to orange.

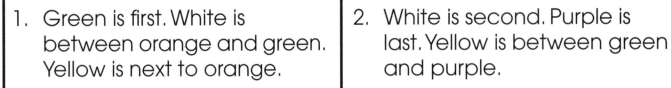

Where is purple? _____

2. White is second. Purple is last. Yellow is between green and purple.

Where is orange? _____

3. White is first. Orange is between white and purple. Yellow is fourth.

Where is green? _____

4. Green is last. Orange is between green and purple. White is second.

Where is yellow? _____

| white | green | yellow | orange | purple |

Bears Night Out

The bears want to camp out.
What night can they both sleep over?
Make a list of the days of the week in
 order to help you.
Circle the day.

1. Today is Sunday. Draw a line under Sunday.
2. Bobby goes to soccer tomorrow night. Put an X.
3. Barry is going fishing on the fourth night of the week. Put an X.
4. Bobby is going to stay with Grandpa the day after tomorrow. Put an X.
5. Barry's mom says no sleepovers on school nights. Put an X.
6. They will put up the tent the day before they camp out. Put an X.

Bear Activities

Look at the pictures below.
Make a ✔ in each correct box.

Bear	Likes to fish	Likes to swim	Likes to read	Likes music
A				
B				
C				
D				

Read.

Write.

1. Which bears like to fish? _____

2. Which bears like to swim? _____

3. Which bear likes to fish and swim? _____

4. Which bears like to read? _____

5. Which bears like to listen to music? _____

6. Which bear likes to read and listen to music? _____

Answer Keys

Page 7

3 < 7	8 > 6	2 < 4
5 > 4	2 < 3	7 > 5
3 < 6	5 > 2	9 > 8
7 < 9	4 > 0	2 < 6

Page 8

5 < 9	6 > 4	2 < 8
6 > 5	9 > 1	8 > 7
2 < 4	1 < 2	5 > 2
9 > 4	3 < 9	1 < 3
6 > 3	5 < 7	8 > 5

Page 9

Sometimes numbers are the same. They are equal.

3 = 3

= means **is the same as.**   Write the numbers above.

8 > 4	0 < 7	4 = 4
3 = 3	6 = 6	7 < 8
5 = 5	2 < 5	6 > 4
7 > 4	3 > 0	9 = 9
6 < 9	2 = 2	4 > 2

Page 10

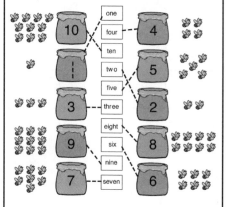

Page 11

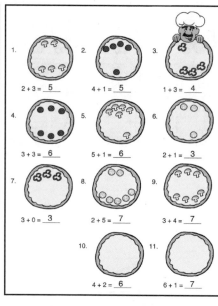

1. $2 + 3 = 5$
2. $4 + 1 = 5$
3. $1 + 3 = 4$
4. $3 + 3 = 6$
5. $5 + 1 = 6$
6. $2 + 1 = 3$
7. $3 + 0 = 3$
8. $2 + 5 = 7$
9. $3 + 4 = 7$
10. $4 + 2 = 6$
11. $6 + 1 = 7$

Page 12

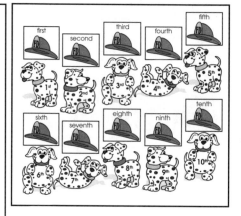

Page 13

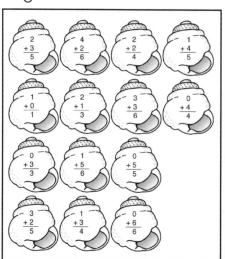

Page 14

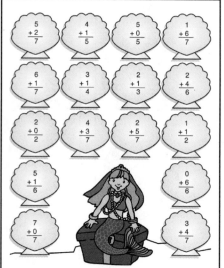

Page 15

$4 + 4 = 8$ $6 + 1 = 7$ $5 + 2 = 7$ $0 + 8 = 8$

$4 + 3 = 7$ $5 + 3 = 8$ $1 + 7 = 8$ $6 + 2 = 8$

$0 + 5 = 5$ $2 + 5 = 7$ $2 + 6 = 8$ $3 + 5 = 8$

$8 + 0 = 8$ $3 + 4 = 7$ $0 + 7 = 7$ $7 + 1 = 8$

Page 17

9 − 3 = 6 (u) 10 − 9 = 1 (w)

9 − 2 = 7 (l) 10 − 6 = 4 (s) 8 − 6 = 2 (o) 10 − 1 = 9 (h)

10 − 7 = 3 (d) 9 − 4 = 5 (t) 10 − 0 = 10 (a) 10 − 2 = 8 (c)

Answer:
t o s e e w h a t
5 2   4   1 9 10 5

h e c o u l d s e e
9   8 2 6 7 3   4

Page 18

6 − 3 = 3 4 − 2 = 2 5 − 4 = 1

5 − 1 = 4 6 − 2 = 4 6 − 5 = 1

6 − 4 = 2 5 − 2 = 3 4 − 3 = 1

Page 19

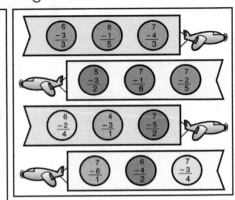

6 − 3 = 3 6 − 1 = 5 7 − 4 = 3

5 − 3 = 2 7 − 1 = 6 7 − 2 = 5

6 − 2 = 4 4 − 3 = 1 7 − 5 = 2

7 − 6 = 1 6 − 4 = 2 7 − 3 = 4

Page 20

8 − 1 = 7 4 − 0 = 4 6 − 3 = 3 8 − 5 = 3

7 − 0 = 7 8 − 2 = 6 6 − 1 = 5 7 − 1 = 6

8 − 4 = 4 7 − 4 = 3 7 − 2 = 5 8 − 3 = 5

Page 21

9 − 6 = 3 8 − 2 = 6 8 − 1 = 7 9 − 4 = 5

8 − 3 = 5 6 − 2 = 4 9 − 0 = 9 9 − 1 = 8

7 − 1 = 6 9 − 2 = 7 7 − 0 = 7 8 − 4 = 4

9 − 5 = 4 9 − 7 = 2 9 − 3 = 6 8 − 0 = 8

Page 22

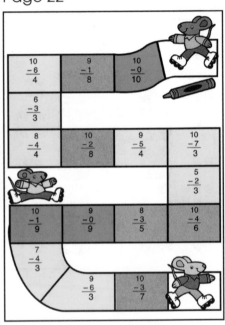

10 − 6 = 4 9 − 1 = 8 10 − 0 = 10

6 − 3 = 3

8 − 4 = 4 10 − 2 = 8 9 − 5 = 4 10 − 7 = 3

5 − 2 = 3

10 − 1 = 9 9 − 0 = 9 8 − 3 = 5 10 − 4 = 6

7 − 4 = 3

9 − 6 = 3 10 − 3 = 7

Page 23

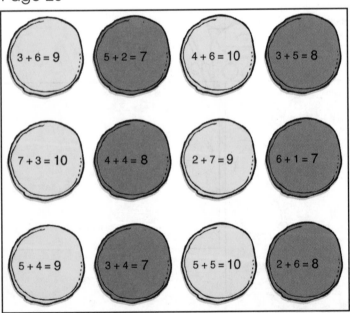

3 + 6 = 9 5 + 2 = 7 4 + 6 = 10 3 + 5 = 8

7 + 3 = 10 4 + 4 = 8 2 + 7 = 9 6 + 1 = 7

5 + 4 = 9 3 + 4 = 7 5 + 5 = 10 2 + 6 = 8

Page 24

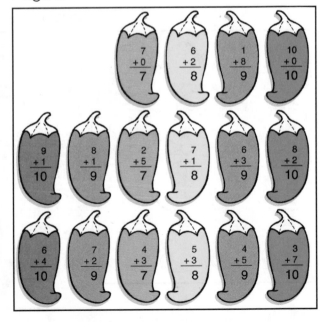

7 + 0 = 7 6 + 2 = 8 1 + 8 = 9 10 + 0 = 10

9 + 1 = 10 8 + 1 = 9 2 + 5 = 7 7 + 1 = 8 6 + 3 = 9 8 + 2 = 10

6 + 4 = 10 7 + 2 = 9 4 + 3 = 7 5 + 3 = 8 4 + 5 = 9 3 + 7 = 10

Page 25

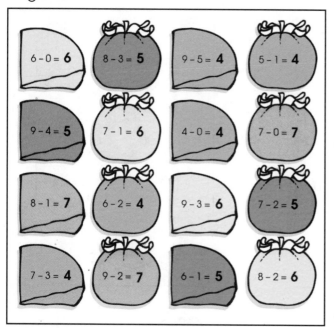

6 – 0 = **6**   8 – 3 = **5**   9 – 5 = **4**   5 – 1 = **4**

9 – 4 = **5**   7 – 1 = **6**   4 – 0 = **4**   7 – 0 = **7**

8 – 1 = **7**   6 – 2 = **4**   9 – 3 = **6**   7 – 2 = **5**

7 – 3 = **4**   9 – 2 = **7**   6 – 1 = **5**   8 – 2 = **6**

Page 26

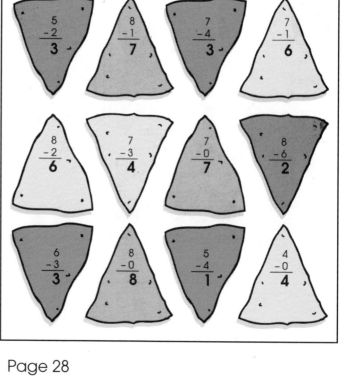

$\begin{array}{r}5\\-2\\\hline 3\end{array}$ $\begin{array}{r}8\\-1\\\hline 7\end{array}$ $\begin{array}{r}7\\-4\\\hline 3\end{array}$ $\begin{array}{r}7\\-1\\\hline 6\end{array}$

$\begin{array}{r}8\\-2\\\hline 6\end{array}$ $\begin{array}{r}7\\-3\\\hline 4\end{array}$ $\begin{array}{r}7\\-0\\\hline 7\end{array}$ $\begin{array}{r}8\\-6\\\hline 2\end{array}$

$\begin{array}{r}6\\-3\\\hline 3\end{array}$ $\begin{array}{r}8\\-0\\\hline 8\end{array}$ $\begin{array}{r}5\\-4\\\hline 1\end{array}$ $\begin{array}{r}4\\-0\\\hline 4\end{array}$

Page 27

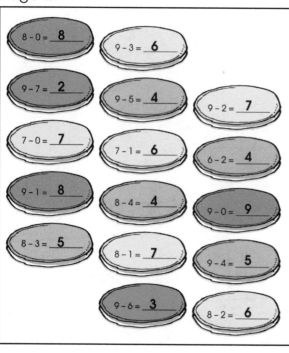

8 – 0 = **8**   9 – 3 = **6**

9 – 7 = **2**   9 – 5 = **4**   9 – 2 = **7**

7 – 0 = **7**   7 – 1 = **6**   6 – 2 = **4**

9 – 1 = **8**   8 – 4 = **4**   9 – 0 = **9**

8 – 3 = **5**   8 – 1 = **7**   9 – 4 = **5**

9 – 6 = **3**   8 – 2 = **6**

Page 28

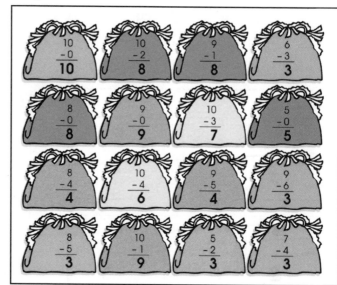

$\begin{array}{r}10\\-0\\\hline 10\end{array}$ $\begin{array}{r}10\\-2\\\hline 8\end{array}$ $\begin{array}{r}9\\-1\\\hline 8\end{array}$ $\begin{array}{r}6\\-3\\\hline 3\end{array}$

$\begin{array}{r}8\\-0\\\hline 8\end{array}$ $\begin{array}{r}9\\-0\\\hline 9\end{array}$ $\begin{array}{r}10\\-3\\\hline 7\end{array}$ $\begin{array}{r}5\\-0\\\hline 5\end{array}$

$\begin{array}{r}8\\-4\\\hline 4\end{array}$ $\begin{array}{r}10\\-4\\\hline 6\end{array}$ $\begin{array}{r}9\\-5\\\hline 4\end{array}$ $\begin{array}{r}9\\-6\\\hline 3\end{array}$

$\begin{array}{r}8\\-5\\\hline 3\end{array}$ $\begin{array}{r}10\\-1\\\hline 9\end{array}$ $\begin{array}{r}5\\-2\\\hline 3\end{array}$ $\begin{array}{r}7\\-4\\\hline 3\end{array}$

Page 29

The ship has 6 sailors.
4 more sailors come aboard.
How many sailors are on the ship?

There are **10** sailors.

There are 5 upper bunk beds.
There are 4 lower bunk beds.
How many bunk beds in all?

There are **9** bunk beds.

**The ship sails to Shell Island to get water.
Add.**

Sal gets 3 jugs of water.
Pete gets 7 jugs of water.
How many jugs in all?

There are **10** jugs of water.

Captain Kidd drinks 5 cups of water.
He drinks 2 more cups of water.
How many cups does he drink?

He drinks **7** cups of water.

The sailors hoist 3 sails.
They hoist 3 more sails.
How many sails are there?

There are **6** sails.

There are 6 boxes of crackers.
There are 2 boxes of jerky.
How many boxes of food in all?

There are **8** boxes.

Ahab gets 4 buckets of water.
Sukey gets 5 buckets of water.
How many buckets in all?

There are **9** buckets.

Pol Parrot takes 8 sips of water.
She takes 1 more sip of water.
How many sips does she take?

She takes **9** sips.

Page 30

Pete sees 10 parrots.
He sees 5 parrots fly away.
How many parrots are left?

There are **5** parrots left.

Jack sees 2 tigers in the grass.
He sees 8 tigers in the bushes.
How many tigers does he see?

Jack sees **10** tigers.

Bill sees 7 monkey babies.
He sees 7 monkey babies run away.
How many babies are left?

There are **0** babies left.

Nell sees 8 snakes.
She sees 4 snakes slide away.
How many snakes are left?

There are **4** snakes left.

Sal sees 6 brown monkeys.
She sees 3 black monkeys.
How many monkeys does she see?

Sal sees **9** monkeys.

Annie sees 9 dolphins.
She sees 7 dolphins swim away.
How many dolphins are left?

There are **2** dolphins left.

Nancy sees 2 baby elephants.
She sees 4 mother elephants.
How many elephants does she see?

Nancy sees **6** elephants.

Tom sees 10 crocodiles.
He sees 2 crocodiles crawl away.
How many crocodiles are left?

There are **8** crocodiles left.

There are 3 monkeys in the trees.   How many monkeys in all?
There are 3 monkeys on the ground.
There are 3 monkeys in the water.   There are **9** monkeys.

Page 31

A sail has 6 holes on one side.
It has 6 holes on the other side.
How many holes are in the sail?

There are **12** holes.

Abby cleans 9 portholes.
Ben cleans 3 portholes.
How many did they clean?

They cleaned **12** portholes.

There are 4 full water jugs.
There are 3 empty water jugs.
How many water jugs in all?

There are **7** water jugs.

There are 3 new mops.
There are 8 old mops.
How many mops in all?

There are **11** mops.

Check the ship's cargo. Fill in the blanks.

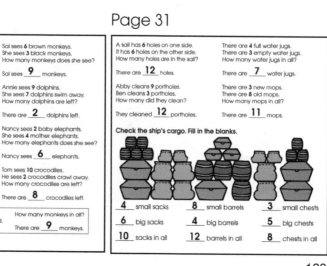

4 small sacks   **8** small barrels   **3** small chests

6 big sacks   **4** big barrels   **5** big chests

10 sacks in all   **12** barrels in all   **8** chests in all

123

Page 32

Page 33

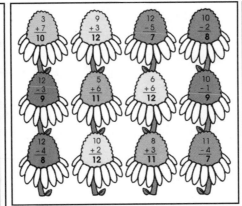

Page 34

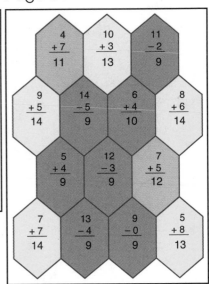

Page 35

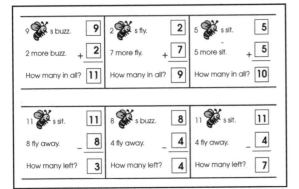

9 bees buzz. **9**	2 bees fly. **2**	5 bees sit. **5**
2 more buzz. + **2**	7 more fly. + **7**	5 more sit. + **5**
How many in all? **11**	How many in all? **9**	How many in all? **10**

11 bees sit. **11**	8 bees buzz. **8**	11 bees sit. **11**
8 fly away. − **8**	4 fly away. − **4**	4 fly away. − **4**
How many left? **3**	How many left? **4**	How many left? **7**

Page 36

She sees 9 bees.	She sees 13 bees.	She sees 7 flowers.
She sees 4 more.	She sees 4 fly away.	She sees 4 more.
She sees **13** bees in all.	She sees **9** bees left.	She sees **11** flowers in all.

She has 12 honeys.	She has 10 flowers.	She has 11 honeys.
She sells 7.	She gets 3 more.	She drops 7.
She has **5** honeys left.	She has **13** flowers in all.	She has **4** honeys left.

Page 37

6 + 7 = **13**	9 + 7 = **16**	
7 + 6 = **13**	7 + 9 = **16**	
13 − 6 = **7**	16 − 9 = **7**	
13 − 7 = **6**	16 − 7 = **9**	
4 + 8 = **12**	8 + 9 = **17**	8 + 7 = **15**
8 + 4 = **12**	9 + 8 = **17**	7 + 8 = **15**
12 − 4 = **8**	17 − 9 = **8**	15 − 7 = **8**
12 − 8 = **4**	17 − 8 = **9**	15 − 8 = **7**

9 + 9 = **18**

18 − 9 = **9**

5 + 7 = **12**

7 + 5 = **12**

12 − 5 = **7**

12 − 7 = **5**

Page 38

Page 39

Page 40

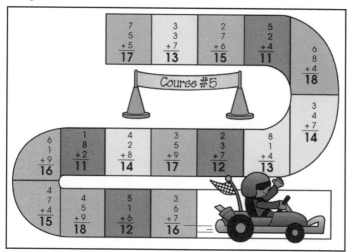

$$\begin{array}{r}7\\5\\+5\\\hline 17\end{array}\quad\begin{array}{r}3\\3\\+7\\\hline 13\end{array}\quad\begin{array}{r}2\\7\\+6\\\hline 15\end{array}\quad\begin{array}{r}5\\2\\+4\\\hline 11\end{array}$$

Course #5

$$\begin{array}{r}6\\8\\+4\\\hline 18\end{array}$$

$$\begin{array}{r}3\\4\\+7\\\hline 14\end{array}$$

$$\begin{array}{r}6\\1\\+9\\\hline 16\end{array}\quad\begin{array}{r}1\\8\\+2\\\hline 11\end{array}\quad\begin{array}{r}4\\2\\+8\\\hline 14\end{array}\quad\begin{array}{r}3\\5\\+9\\\hline 17\end{array}\quad\begin{array}{r}2\\3\\+7\\\hline 12\end{array}\quad\begin{array}{r}8\\1\\+4\\\hline 13\end{array}$$

$$\begin{array}{r}4\\7\\+4\\\hline 15\end{array}\quad\begin{array}{r}4\\5\\+9\\\hline 18\end{array}\quad\begin{array}{r}5\\1\\+6\\\hline 12\end{array}\quad\begin{array}{r}3\\6\\+7\\\hline 16\end{array}$$

Page 41

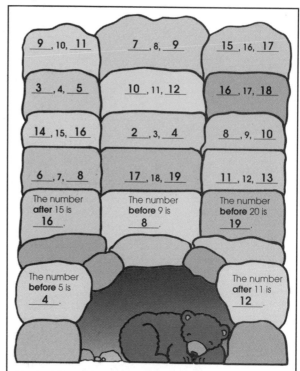

9, 10, __11__   7, __8__, 9   15, 16, __17__

__3__, 4, __5__   __10__, 11, 12   __16__, 17, __18__

__14__, 15, __16__   __2__, 3, __4__   __8__, 9, __10__

__6__, 7, __8__   __17__, 18, __19__   __11__, 12, __13__

The number after 15 is __16__.

The number before 9 is __8__.

The number before 20 is __19__.

The number before 5 is __4__.

The number after 11 is __12__.

Page 43

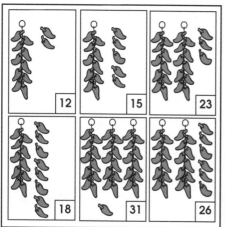

| 12 | 15 | 23 |
| 18 | 31 | 26 |

Page 44

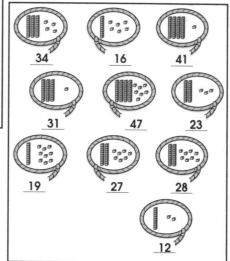

34   16   41

31   47   23

19   27   28

12

Page 46

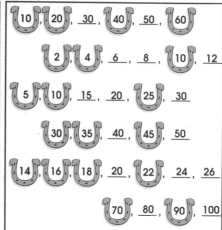

10, 20, __30__, 40, __50__, 60

2, 4, __6__, __8__, __10__, __12__

5, 10, __15__, __20__, __25__, __30__

30, 35, __40__, __45__, __50__

14, 16, 18, __20__, __22__, __24__, __26__

70, __80__, __90__, __100__

Page 54

Three friends will share the 9 goody bags. How many will each friend get?

3

Liz has 6 cupcakes. She wants to share half of them with her friend Suzi. How many cupcakes will Liz have left?

3

Chris has 8 balloons. He wants to share them with his friend Darcy. How many balloons will Chris and Darcy each have?

4

Molly had 3 friends over to play. Molly had 12 dolls for her friends to play with. If each friend had an equal number of dolls, how many dolls did each one get?

4

Page 63

3 pounds   5 pounds

9 pounds   1 pounds

2 pounds   8 pounds

Page 68

1. The first day of this month is on **Thursday**
2. The last day of this month is on **Saturday**
3. The day after Thursday is **Friday**

Answer each question by matching it with a number.

1. How many days are in the month? — 16
2. How many Thursdays are in the month? — 31
3. What date is Dan's birthday? — 5
4. What was the date when it began to snow? — 4
5. What was the first sunny date in the month? — 22

Page 74

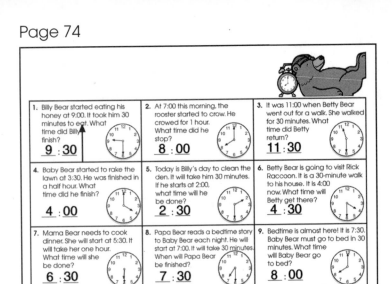

1. Billy Bear started eating his honey at 9:00. It took him 30 minutes to eat. What time did Billy finish?
9:**30**

2. At 7:00 this morning, the rooster started to crow. He crowed for 1 hour. What time did he stop?
8:**00**

3. It was 11:00 when Betty Bear went out for a walk. She walked for 30 minutes. What time did Betty return?
11:**30**

4. Baby Bear started to rake the lawn at 3:30. He was finished in a half hour. What time did he finish?
4:**00**

5. Today is Billy's day to clean the den. It will take him 30 minutes. If he starts at 2:00, what time will he be done?
2:**30**

6. Betty Bear is going to visit Rick Raccoon. It is a 30-minute walk to his house. It is 4:00 now. What time will Betty get there?
4:**30**

7. Mama Bear needs to cook dinner. She will start at 5:30. It will take her one hour. What time will she be done?
6:**30**

8. Papa Bear reads a bedtime story to Baby Bear each night. He will start at 7:00. It will take 30 minutes. When will Papa Bear be finished?
7:**30**

9. Bedtime is almost here! It is 7:30. Baby Bear must go to bed in 30 minutes. What time will Baby Bear go to bed?
8:**00**

Page 79

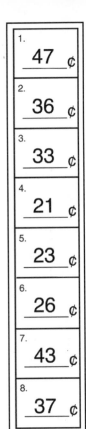

1. **47** ¢
2. **36** ¢
3. **33** ¢
4. **21** ¢
5. **23** ¢
6. **26** ¢
7. **43** ¢
8. **37** ¢

Page 80

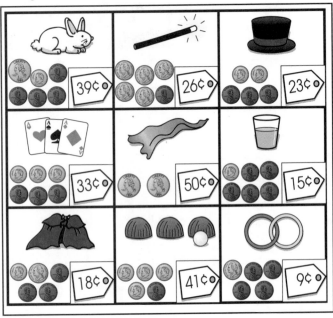

39¢ | 26¢ | 23¢
33¢ | 50¢ | 15¢
18¢ | 41¢ | 9¢

Page 81

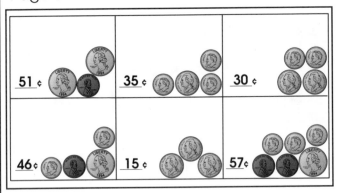

51 ¢ | **35** ¢ | **30** ¢
46 ¢ | **15** ¢ | **57** ¢

Page 86

Shape	Number of Sides	Number of Corners
triangle	3	3
square	4	4
circle	0	0
rectangle	4	4
hexagon	6	6
trapezoid	4	4

Page 97

Stars	Answer
10 5 20 15	_5_ _10_ _15_ _20_
4 2 8 6	_2_ _4_ _6_ _8_
7 3 5 9	_3_ _5_ _7_ _9_
20 10 30 40	_10_ _20_ _30_ _40_
45 35 30 40	_30_ _35_ _40_ _45_
12 16 14 18	_12_ _14_ _16_ _18_

Page 98

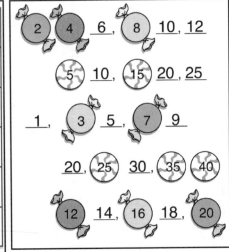

2 4 _6_ 8 _10_, _12_

_5_ 10 _15_ _20_, _25_

_1_, 3 _5_, 7 _9_

_20_, 25 _30_, 35 _40_

12 _14_, 16 _18_, 20

Page 99

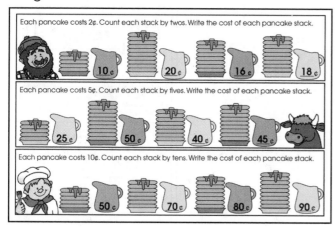

Each pancake costs 2¢. Count each stack by twos. Write the cost of each pancake stack.

10¢   20¢   16¢   18¢

Each pancake costs 5¢. Count each stack by fives. Write the cost of each pancake stack.

25¢   50¢   40¢   45¢

Each pancake costs 10¢. Count each stack by tens. Write the cost of each pancake stack.

50¢   70¢   80¢   90¢

Page 100

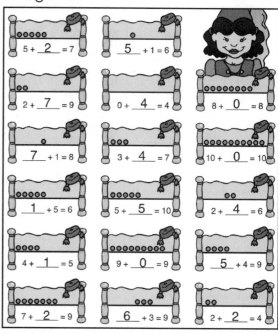

$5 + \underline{2} = 7$ $\underline{5} + 1 = 6$

$2 + \underline{7} = 9$ $0 + \underline{4} = 4$ $8 + \underline{0} = 8$

$\underline{7} + 1 = 8$ $3 + \underline{4} = 7$ $10 + \underline{0} = 10$

$\underline{1} + 5 = 6$ $5 + \underline{5} = 10$ $2 + \underline{4} = 6$

$4 + \underline{1} = 5$ $9 + \underline{0} = 9$ $\underline{5} + 4 = 9$

$7 + \underline{2} = 9$ $\underline{6} + 3 = 9$ $2 + \underline{2} = 4$

Page 101

+ 10	
6	16
3	13
2	12

− 4	
10	6
8	4
12	8

+ 7	
6	13
5	12
9	16

+ 5	
10	15
7	12
4	9

− 2	
6	4
9	7
10	8

− 3	
4	1
7	4
6	3

− 1	
8	7
10	9
3	2

+ 4	
7	11
6	10
1	5

Page 106

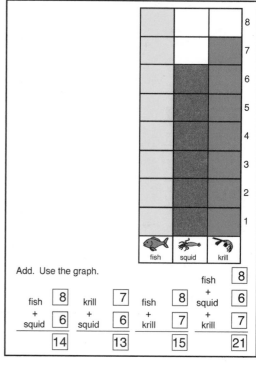

Add. Use the graph.

fish 8
+ squid 6
14

krill 7
+ squid 6
13

fish 8
+ krill 7
15

fish 8
+ squid 6
+ krill 7
21

Page 107

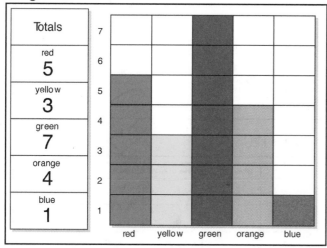

Totals	
red	5
yellow	3
green	7
orange	4
blue	1

red   yellow   green   orange   blue

Page 108

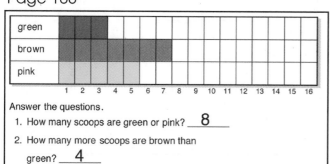

	1	2	3	4	5	6	7	8	9	10	11	12	13	14	15	16
green																
brown																
pink																

Answer the questions.

1. How many scoops are green or pink? __8__

2. How many more scoops are brown than green? __4__

Page 109

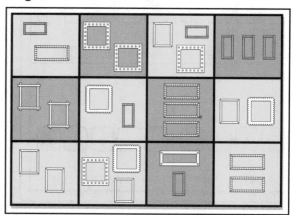

Page 110

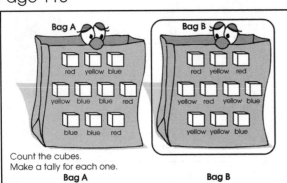

Count the cubes.
Make a tally for each one.

Bag A

Color	Tally Marks
red	|||
blue	ⵀⵏ
yellow	||

Bag B

Color	Tally Marks
red	|||
blue	||
yellow	ⵀⵏ

Answer the questions.

Which bag has more yellow cubes? **B**

Which bag has fewer yellow cubes? **A**

Page 112

Page 113

Page 114

Sam has 2 gumballs. Ted gave him 2 more. How many does he have now? **4**	Emily had 5 flowers. She gave 3 of them to Sarah. How many flowers are left? **2**
Chris has 3 goldfish. Mark has 4 goldfish. How many goldfish in all? **7**	Missy found 6 rocks. Darcy found 3 rocks. How many rocks in all? **9**
Jake got 2 balloons at the fair. Carly got 6 balloons at the fair. How many balloons in all? **8**	Amy gave Mike 4 balls. She had 10 to begin with. How many balls does Amy have left? **6**

Page 116

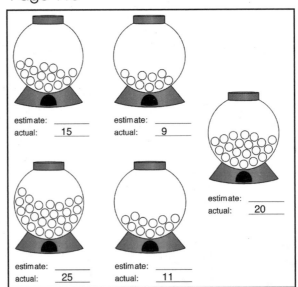

estimate: _____
actual: **15**

estimate: _____
actual: **9**

estimate: _____
actual: **20**

estimate: _____
actual: **25**

estimate: _____
actual: **11**

Page 118

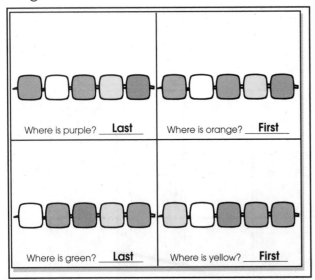

Where is purple? **Last**

Where is orange? **First**

Where is green? **Last**

Where is yellow? **First**

Page 120

Bear	Likes to fish	Likes to swim	Likes to read	Likes music
A	✔			✔
B	✔	✔		
C		✔	✔	
D			✔	✔

Read.
Write.

1. Which bears like to fish? **A, B**
2. Which bears like to swim? **B, C**
3. Which bear likes to fish and swim? **B**
4. Which bears like to read? **C, D**
5. Which bears like to listen to music? **A, D**
6. Which bear likes to read and listen to music? **D**